BAPTISTWAY

# Bible Study for Texas

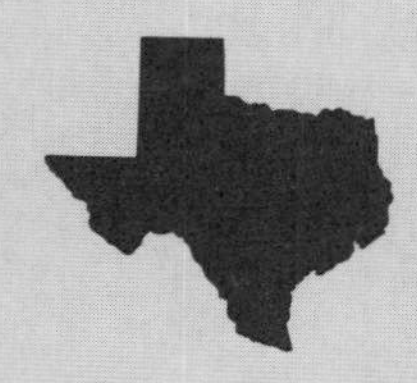

# The Gospel of Luke

*Meeting Jesus Again, Anew*

Paul Powell
Leroy Kemp
Leroy Fenton

BAPTISTWAY
Dallas, Texas

Bible Study for Texas, The Gospel of Luke: Meeting Jesus Again, Anew



Printed in the United States of America.



BAPTISTWAY Management Team
Executive Director, Baptist General Convention of Texas: William M. Pinson, Jr.
Director, State Missions Commission: James Semple
Director, Sunday School/Discipleship Division: Bernard M. Spooner

Publishing consultant: Ross West, Positive Difference Communications
Cover and Interior Design and Production: Desktop Miracles, Inc.

First edition: March 2000.

ISBN: 0–9673424–0–6

# How to Make the Best Use of Bible Study for Texas

## Whether you're the teacher or a student—

1. Start early in the week before your class meets.
2. Overview the study. Look at the table of contents, read the study introduction, and read the unit introduction for the lesson you're about to study. Try to see how each lesson relates to the unit and overall study of which it is a part.
3. Use your Bible to read and consider prayerfully the Scripture passages for the lesson. (You'll see that each writer has chosen a favorite translation for each unit. You're free to use the Bible translation you prefer and compare it with the translation chosen, of course.)
4. After reading all the Scripture passages in your Bible, then read the writer's comments. The comments are intended to be an aid to your study of the Bible.
5. Read the small articles—"sidebars"—in each lesson. They are intended to provide additional, enrichment information and inspiration and to encourage thought and application.
6. Try to answer for yourself the questions included in each lesson. They're intended to encourage further thought and application, and they can also be used in the class session itself.

## If you're the teacher—

A. Do all of the things just mentioned, of course.

B. In the first session of the study, briefly overview the study by identifying with your class the date on which each lesson will be studied. Lead your class to write the date in the table of contents on page 5 and on the first page of each lesson.

C. You may want to get the enrichment teaching help that is provided in the *Baptist Standard* and/or on the Internet. Call 214–630–4571 to begin your subscription to the *Baptist Standard*. Send an e-mail to baptistway@bgct.org to find out how to access the Internet information. (Other class participants may find this information helpful, too.)

D. Get a copy of the *Teaching Guide*, which is a companion piece to these lesson comments. The teaching suggestions in the *Teaching Guide* are intended to provide practical, easy-to-use teaching suggestions that will work in your class.
E. After you've studied the Bible passage, the lesson contents, and other material, use the teaching suggestions in the *Teaching Guide* to help you develop your plan for leading your class in studying each lesson.
F. Enjoy leading your class in discovering the meaning of the Scripture passages and in applying these passages to their lives.

# The Gospel of Luke: Meeting Jesus Again, Anew

UNIT THREE

## *Getting Your Priorities Straight*

**Date of Study**

# Introducing
## *The Gospel of Luke: Meeting Jesus Again, Anew*

So what is Jesus really like? Evidently that's a question that a first-century Christian named Luke wanted to help people answer. The Gospel of Luke begins with the statement that many before him had tried to "compile an account of the things accomplished among us, just as they were handed down to us by those who from the beginning were eyewitnesses and servants of the word" (Luke 1:1–2, NASB[1]). Now, however, to Luke, having "carefully investigated everything from the beginning, it seemed good also . . . to write an orderly account" (1:3, NIV[2]).

Luke wrote his account, the Gospel of Luke, to Theophilus. We may make some good, educated guesses about the identity of Theophilus, but we really know nothing for sure about him except that his name means "lover of God." What a great name! Could that name describe you?

When the Gospel of Luke first appeared and began to be read, perhaps fifty years had passed since Jesus had lived, died, been resurrected, and ascended. Luke was reminding people who had lived through those days of the meaning of all that Jesus had done. Luke was also reminding people who had not participated in those events of how that meaning spoke to them and to their church.

As with the other gospels, the Gospel of Luke has its own special emphases. These emphases radiate from the portrait that Luke paints of Jesus. In Luke's Gospel we can hear, in effect, this invitation from Jesus: *Come to the party God is having, all of you. Yes, I really mean you.* Luke's Gospel pictures Jesus breaking down the barriers that separated people. Luke shows Jesus reaching out to all people, which means to all kinds of people. In Luke, Jesus demonstrated special concern for people who were considered second-class in one way or another. Included in this definition were people who didn't keep the Jewish traditions, people whom the religious leaders considered sinners. Included as well were people who were in fact sinners. Other people considered second-class were the poor, the oppressed, and women. Jesus affirmed and reached out in love and acceptance to them all.

The Gospel of Luke also places strong emphasis on social justice and is especially concerned for the poor and the oppressed. This emphasis can be seen in the first lesson of this study—on Jesus' sermon at the synagogue in Nazareth (Luke 4:14–30)—as well as at other points (see 1:46–55; 6:20–21; 7:11–17).

Luke invited his readers to meet Jesus afresh and anew. If we let the message of Luke's Gospel get through to us, we also may well see Jesus in a fresh, new way. The Scriptures selected for study are intended to help you understand and apply the thrust of the Gospel of Luke to your life. These passages provide teachings related to the priorities and values of Texas Baptists. The study also emphasizes those passages unique to the Gospel of Luke, the incidents and teachings that appear only in Luke and that thus provide insight into Luke's special message about Jesus.

The study follows generally the order of Luke's Gospel, with two exceptions. One adjustment in order, lesson seven, is a lesson on Jesus' resurrection. Such a lesson is appropriate for study at any time, but it is placed here especially for use on Easter of the first year of release of this volume of *Bible Study for Texas*. When Luke is studied at other times, classes may choose whether to study lesson seven at this point or as the final lesson of the study. Another adjustment is in lesson eight, which includes a passage from Luke 5 along with a passage in Luke 14 on a related subject.

## NOTES

1. NASB refers to the New American Standard Bible, Copyright © The Lockman Foundation 1960, 1962, 1963, 1968, 1971, 1972, 1973, 1975, 1977, 1995.
2. NIV refers to the *Holy Bible: New International Version*. Copyright © 1973, 1978, 1984, by the International Bible Society. Published by Zondervan Bible Publishers.
3. Listing a book does not imply full agreement by the writers or BAPTISTWAY with all of its comments.

These commentaries may provide additional help for this study. The resources are listed in alphabetical order.[3]

William Barclay. *The Gospel of Luke.* The Daily Study Bible. Revised edition. Philadephia: The Westminster Press, 1956.

Darrell L. Bock. "Luke." *The NIV Application Commentary*. Grand Rapids, Michigan: Zondervan Publishing House, 1996.

Fred B. Craddock. *Luke*. Interpretation. Louisville: John Knox Press, 1990.

R. Alan Culpepper. "The Gospel of Luke." *The New Interpreter's Bible*. Volume IX. Nashville: Abingdon Press, 1995.

Herschel H. Hobbs. *An Exposition of the Gospel of Luke.* Baker Book House, Grand Rapids, 1966.

Leon Morris. *Luke*. Tyndale New Testament Commentaries. Leicester, England: IVP, 1974.

Robert H. Stein. *Luke*. The New American Commentary. Volume 24. Nashville, Tennessee: Broadman Press, 1992.

Ray Summers. *Commentary on Luke: Jesus, the Universal Savior*. Waco, Texas: Word Books, 1972.

Malcolm Tolbert. "The Gospel of Luke." *The Broadman Bible Commentary*. Volume 9. Nashville, Tennessee: Broadman Press, 1970.

UNIT 1

# Our Response to Jesus' Mission

A noted historian is said to have been asked which person he thought had left the most permanent impression on history. His answer was that if a person's greatness were judged by historical standards, Jesus Christ would stand first.

We're bound to ask of a person so prominent, "Who is Jesus? What did he do?" Clues to the identity and redemptive mission of Jesus are found in the gospels—Matthew, Mark, Luke, and John.

The gospels are not biographies in the strictest sense. They are sketches. They tell us of Jesus' birth, his public ministry, and his death, but they devote only a few lines to his formative years. Luke tells us that he was circumcised on the eighth day and that his family made a pilgrimage to Jerusalem when he was twelve years of age, but beyond that we know nothing of his childhood and youth. We don't even know how he looked.

After telling of Jesus' birth and giving only a glimpse of Jesus' childhood, Luke shows Jesus appearing as a fully-grown man ready to enter his public ministry. Approximately one-third of each of the four gospels is devoted to the last week of Jesus' life. Clearly the focal point of the writers was on the fact that Jesus came to die.

Who is Jesus? He is the Son of God. Jesus is not just another good man finding his way to God. He is God himself finding his way to people (Luke 1:35).

Why did Jesus come? He came to be our Savior and the Savior of the whole world (see Luke 2:11).

This series of lessons deals with our response to Jesus and his mission. It is only as we understand who he is and why he came that we can respond appropriately to him.

# LUKE: Meeting Jesus Again, Anew

In this series of four lessons, we will:

- see Jesus extending God's grace to all people (Luke 4:16–27)
- hear his call to follow him in discipleship (Luke 5:1–11, 27–28)
- learn to live as forgiven people (Luke 7:36–50)
- realize that Jesus wants to send us as he sent his first disciples to do God's work in the world (Luke 10:1–17)

## Focal Text

Luke 4:16–27

## Background

Luke 4:14–30

## Main Focus

Jesus' ministry extends God's grace to all people.

## Question to Explore

What is the good news Jesus brings, and for whom is it intended?

## Study Aim

To evaluate how well I share the gospel so as to extend God's grace to all people

## Texas Priorities Emphasized

- Share the gospel of Jesus Christ with the people of Texas, the nation and the world
- Minister to human needs in the name of Jesus Christ
- Equip people for ministry in the church and in the world

LESSON ONE

# Extending God's Grace to All People

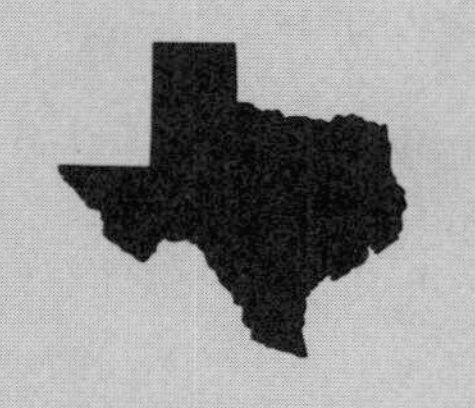

## Quick Read

Jesus began his public ministry in his hometown of Nazareth by announcing that he was the Messiah promised in the Old Testament Scriptures and that he had come to extend God's grace to all people.

Viktor Frankl, a psychiatrist who survived the horrors and atrocities of a Nazi concentration camp during World War II, said one reason he was able to do so was because he discovered a reason for living. Following his liberation from prison camp, he developed a new school of psychological thought built on the conviction that a person's life is basically a search for meaning. And, he said, the person who has a "why" to live for can bear with almost any "how."[1]

Thinkers everywhere agree that one of the most dominant needs of all people is meaning in life—a purpose for being. One of the reasons Jesus' life exuded such confidence and authority is that he knew who he was, why he was here, and where he was going. His confidence was cemented in the knowledge that his purpose was always to do the will of the Father.

Jesus expressed that will, that purpose, that mission on earth when he announced:

> The Spirit of the Lord is upon Me,
> Because He anointed Me to preach the gospel to the poor.
> He has sent Me to proclaim release to the captives,
> And recovery of sight to the blind,
> To set free those who are oppressed,
> To proclaim the favorable year of the Lord.
> (Luke 4:18–19, NASB)

The occasion for this statement was Jesus' first visit to his hometown of Nazareth after he had begun his public ministry. His fame as a preacher and miracle worker had already been established and had spread rapidly. Now he was back for a visit to the town where he had grown up. As was his custom, he went to the synagogue to worship on the Sabbath day.

---

## Nazareth

We make a mistake if we think of Jesus being brought up in a village. His hometown of Nazareth was called a *polis*, which means a town or city (Luke 2:4). It may well have had as many as twenty thousand inhabitants. One great road stretched north and south, and on it traveled pilgrims making their way to the Temple in Jerusalem. Stretching east and west was the great road traveled by the caravans from Arabia and by Roman legions marching out to the eastern frontier of the empire. So Jesus grew up in a city surrounded by history and with the traffic of the world at its doors almost continually.

---

The leader of the synagogue asked him to read the Scriptures and to deliver the sermon. He took the scroll of the prophet Isaiah, turned to what we know as Isaiah 61:1–2, and read to the congregation. This passage is a prophecy concerning the Messiah. When Jesus had finished reading this prophecy, he sat down and said to the congregation, "Today this Scripture has been fulfilled in your hearing" (Luke 4:21, NASB).

Jesus thus declared to them that he was the Messiah whom Isaiah had predicted. He was the Savior for whom they had longed. This passage in Isaiah tells us clearly why Jesus came.

*In these four words—emancipation, illumination, liberation, and salvation—we have an answer as to why Jesus came initially. They also tell us what he can and will do for us today if we will follow him.*

Jesus' message met with a good response from his hearers until he suggested that God's good news was for all people, not just for the Jews. He did this by using two illustrations from the Old Testament. One was from the life of Elijah, and the other was from the life of Elisha. There were many Jewish widows in Elijah's day. But the only widow God miraculously sustained and used to sustain his prophet was the widow of Zarephath. She was a non-Jew from the land of Sidon. Too, there were many Jewish lepers in Elisha's day, but the only one who had been healed was Naaman the Syrian, also a non-Jew.

When the people heard Jesus' message, they were so enraged they tried to throw Jesus from the cliff on which the city was built. They would have done so if they could have.

This passage teaches us two things we need to know about God's grace: It encompasses all needs, and it extends to all people.

## He Meets All Our Needs

Luke 4:18–19 sets out four reasons for Jesus' coming.

- He came for emanicipation—"to proclaim release to the captives."
- He came for illumination—to restore "sight to the blind."
- He came for liberation—"to set free those who are oppressed."
- He came for salvation—"to proclaim the favorable year of the Lord."

In these four words—emancipation, illumination, liberation, and salvation—we have an answer as to why Jesus came initially. They also tell us what he can and will do for us today if we will follow him.

Why did Jesus come? What was his overriding mission on earth?

Jesus came first for emancipation: He came "to proclaim release to the captives" (4:18, NASB). These captives were not and are not people in jail. They were and are people in the bondage of sin. As Jesus said elsewhere, "Everyone who commits sin is the slave of sin" (John 8:34, NASB).

*We can be free persons. We can know liberty in Jesus Christ. This is one of the reasons he came.*

The tyranny of sin can be seen everywhere. Lust is a tyrant. Greed is a tyrant. Superstition is a tyrant. Anger is a tyrant. Ambition is a tyrant. Sin is a master that enslaves people apart from Christ.

We all know that the drunkard becomes a slave to alcohol and the drug addict becomes hooked on drugs. But the perfectionist can become so in love with details that he or she becomes cruel and irritable with those who have not a love for completeness.

Everywhere people have bad habits they can't seem to break. They want to be free from these things. In fact, they may have said a thousand times that they are going to change, but they never do.

The story is told that the Persian king Darius once sprained his foot while out hunting. Darius retained at his court the most distinguished members of the medical profession. Their treatment, however, only aggravated the condition of his foot. The king spent seven sleepless days and nights. Finally, someone told him of a certain Democedes of Croton who had unusual medical skills. Democedes was a slave. He was brought into the king's presence, trailing chains and clad in rags. Democedes was able to soothe the king's foot and promote its healing. As a reward, Darius gave Democedes two pairs of golden fetters. His bondage continued; his chains were just more expensive and more attractive.

*The one who holds the stars in heaven also reaches down to lift us up when life comes crushing in upon us.*

Sin is like that. It leads eventually to bondage. Sometimes its chains are of iron, sometimes they are of gold, but the same enslavement results. The only difference is the price of the chains.

Jesus, however, can set us free. We no longer need to live in slavery to Satan and wrongdoing. We can be free persons. We can know liberty in Jesus Christ. This is one of the reasons he came.

Jesus came also for illumination. He came for "recovery of sight to the blind." There are two kinds of blindness in the Bible—physical blindness and spiritual blindness. Handel, after he had written the *Messiah*, went blind. But he confessed that his ability to see Christ increased as his ability to see others decreased.

Jesus restored the sight of many people who were physically blind, but he primarily came to give sight to those who were spiritually blind. As a result of Christ's coming, many people have seen themselves, God, eternity, and others clearly for the first time.

It's possible for a person to have poor vision and not know it. That happened to me. When I was in college, I was having a difficult time seeing the chalkboard. I thought it was just because of the glare from the window. I thought everybody was having the same problem I was. Then one day I was at a baseball game with a friend. He made a comment about a sign on the centerfield fence. I asked, "Can you read that sign?" He said, "Sure I can. Can't you?" I said, "I can't read a word of it." He said, "Man, you must be

---

## The Synagogue

Jesus' ministry began in the synagogue. The synagogue was the real center of religious life in Palestine in Jesus' day. Synagogues did not originate until the Babylonian captivity and exile (about 597–538 B.C.). The captivity and exile came because of Israel's idolatry and lasted seventy years. As is often the case, good things came out of this bad experience. At least three positive results came out of the captivity. First, it cured Israel of idolatry. Never again would they worship other gods. Second, the Jews learned commerce from the Babylonians and forever after would be known as great merchants. Third, separated from their homeland and with their Temple destroyed by Babylon, they developed local houses of worship called synagogues. There was only one Temple, but the law said that wherever there were ten Jewish families there must be a synagogue. And so in every town and village it was in the synagogue that people met to worship. There were no sacrifices in the synagogue. The Temple was for sacrifice; the synagogue was for teaching.

The synagogue service had three parts. First, worship. Prayer was offered. Second, reading. People from the congregation were selected to read passages from the law and the prophets. Third, teaching. Instruction was given.

In the synagogue there was no professional ministry; there was no one person to give the sermon. The leader of the synagogue would invite any distinguished person present to speak, and then a discussion and talk would follow.

That is how Jesus got his chance to speak in the synagogue. The synagogue became a platform that was open for him to announce his mission and ministry for the first time.

---

blind." So I went to the optometrist, and sure enough, I needed glasses. I had a vision problem, and I didn't even know it until then.

Many people today are in the same condition spiritually. They do not see their own sinfulness. They have never caught a glimpse of the glory of God. They have no vision of eternity. They grope in spiritual darkness, blinded by Satan, the god of this world. But Jesus can open their eyes to spiritual reality (see John 8:12). If we come to him, he can give sight to the blind. That's a part of why he came.

Jesus also came for liberation: He came to "set free those who are oppressed" (Luke 4:18, NASB). Oppression is different from slavery. It carries with it a sense of being crushed, defeated, and whipped down by life.

Many people are not only bound by their habits but are crushed by their circumstances, their emotions, their attitudes, and their outlook. They need to be liberated from fear and worry, from depression and loneliness, from pessimism and doubt, as well as from their sinful appetites.

Ernest Hemingway, one of the most celebrated writers ever to pick up a pen, once lamented that he felt as if he lived in a vacuum and was as lonely as a radio tube when the batteries had gone dead and there was no current to plug in to. Then he put a shotgun to his head and pulled the trigger.

A young lady who had just gone through a divorce came to me for counseling. She said, "Since Bill didn't want me I just decided that nobody wanted me." That kind of loneliness and despair, meaninglessness and misery, crushes people everywhere. Jesus came for such oppressed and downtrodden people. He came to help us overcome our inferior feelings, our bad attitudes, our negative outlooks. The one who holds the stars in heaven also reaches down to lift us up when life comes crushing in upon us.

---

## Jesus' Religious Life

This visit of Jesus to the synagogue reveals two significant things about Jesus' religious life. One, he made a habit of regular worship. He went to the synagogue "as was His custom" (Luke 4:16, NASB). Two, he knew the Scriptures. When called on to read, he immediately turned to the passage he wanted. The Scriptures in those days were written on long scrolls. Jesus did not have the benefit of marked chapters and verses as our Bibles have today. Obviously, Jesus was very familiar with God's word to be able to find his way to the correct passage so readily.

---

Fourth, Jesus came for salvation: "To proclaim the favorable year of the Lord" (verse 19, NASB). He came to announce that the day of salvation had come. God's offer, God's promise, God's provision, is now available. If you will receive it today, salvation can be yours.

If Christ had not come to die for our sins, we would not have had the chance to be saved. Because he came, all people can be saved.

Why did Jesus come? What was his mission? He came to set us free from the bondage of our sins, to open our eyes to see both time and eternity, to set us free from the circumstances, emotions, and attitudes that beat us down, and to announce that the day of salvation has come.

*God's offer, God's promise, God's provision, is now available. If you will receive it today, salvation can be yours.*

If you have a broken heart, come to Jesus. If you are gripped by unbreakable habits, come to Jesus. If you're bound and blinded by a negative outlook or a bad attitude, come to Jesus. If you are oppressed and depressed by life, come to Jesus. If you're lost and want to be found, come to Jesus. His salvation encompasses all our need.

## Extended to All People

Jesus' sermon was well received until he used the two illustrations, one from the life of Elijah and the other from the life of Elisha. Both indicated that God's grace not only encompassed all needs but it was extended to all people. Both illustrations pointed to God's favor and blessings to non-Jews.

In the days of Elijah, there were many needy widows in the land. But when the Lord wanted to care for his prophet, he sent him to a non-Jewish woman from the land of Sidon who had the faith to believe the man of God (see 1 Kings 17:8–16).

And there were many lepers who needed cleansing in Elisha's day. But the only one who received cleansing from God was a non-Jew, a leper named Naaman from Syria who had faith to believe the word of God (see 2 Kings 5:1–14).

Don't miss the fact that these two people were of different genders—one a woman, one a man. They were of two different classes—one a lowly widow and one a high government official. They were of two different nations—Sidon and Syria. And they had two different needs—one needed food, the other needed healing. The one common denominator was their faith. They believed and acted on God's word from God's messenger when it came to them. Thus they were the lone recipients of God's grace.

The compliments Jesus paid to Gentiles angered the people. The Jews of Jesus' day were so sure that they were God's people that they utterly despised all other people. Here, however, was Jesus, whom they all had known from his childhood, preaching as if the Gentiles were equally favored by God. It was beginning to dawn on them that there were things in the new message the like of which they had never dreamed of. What the Messiah had come to do he had come to do for all people, not just for the Jews.

*This experience of Jesus teaches us clearly that God's grace is inclusive, not exclusive.*

In one of his last interviews before he died, the poet Carl Sandburg is said to have been asked whether there were any bad words in the English language. His response was that to his knowledge there was only one, the word "exclusive." To be exclusive means that you feel superior to and therefore regard others as unworthy of your association and friendship. There were many people in Jesus' day who were sinfully exclusive. We have not moved beyond that in our day. We still tend to think that God's blessings are only for us and for our kind.

This experience of Jesus teaches us clearly that God's grace is inclusive, not exclusive. It encompasses all needs, and it is extended to all people. Jesus' mission and message is for all people, regardless of race or class or gender, who will respond to it in faith.

## For Thought and Action

- Everybody has a problem, is a problem, or lives near one. The scope of Jesus' ministry therefore applies to all of us.
- Many people feel excluded from the circle of God's love for many reasons. We need to reach out to them and let them know that God's grace is for them also.
- Pride, indifference, and exclusiveness exist in every community and unfortunately every church. They need to be rooted out and replaced by love.
- There are ways in which all of us can reach out to the poor, the downtrodden, and the oppressed of the world. We need to explore and to begin to utilize those means.

## QUESTIONS

1. In what way has Jesus set you free from sin? opened your eyes to new truth? lifted you up from oppression or depression?

2. Do you know of some acquaintance who needs the emancipation, the illumination, the liberation, and the salvation Jesus came to bring?

3. In what ways are we religiously exclusive today?

4. Who are some people in your community who are generally excluded from your church? Are they people who need to be reached with God's grace?

5. What ideas do you have as to how to reach them?

6. What does Jesus' sermon suggest to you about God's concern for the poor and the oppressed?

## NOTES

1. Viktor E. Frankl, *Man's Search for Meaning*, rev. ed. (New York: Washington Square Press, 1984), 101.

## Focal Text

Luke 5:1–11, 27–28

## Background

Luke 5:1–28

## Main Focus

Jesus calls us to leave everything else and follow him.

## Question to Explore

What does Jesus ask of me?

## Study Aim

To identify what Jesus is calling me to do

## Texas Priorities Emphasized

- Share the gospel of Jesus Christ with the people of Texas, the nation and the world
- Minister to human needs in the name of Jesus Christ
- Equip people for ministry in the church and in the world

# LESSON TWO Responding to Jesus' Call

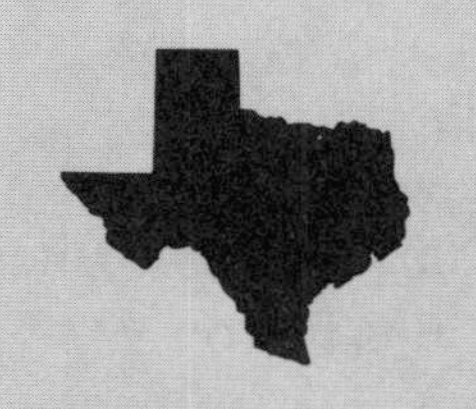

## Quick Read

From the outset of his ministry, Jesus called people to join him in his great effort to reach the world. They needed simply to follow him in obedience and discipleship, and he would make them what they should become. It is as if Jesus were saying, "Give me twelve ordinary people who will forsake all and follow me, and I will turn the world upside down."

A young person is said to have gone to see John D. Rockefeller to apply for a job. Rockefeller asked the young man whether he was a leader. The young man quickly responded by saying that he was not a leader, but he certainly was a good follower.

Amused, Mr. Rockefeller responded by hiring the young man on the spot. He told the boy he had scores of employees who fancied themselves to be leaders. He was sure he could use at least one good follower.

*. . . We must get outside the church if we're going to reach the unchurched.*

The one clear call of Jesus to people during his earthly ministry was the call "follow me." That call comes to us, too. It is presented to us clearly in two experiences found in the fifth chapter of the Gospel of Luke.

In today's lesson, we are confronted with a turning point in the ministry of Jesus. In the previous lesson we heard him preach in the synagogue. When Jesus indicated that he had come to be the Savior of all people, not just the Jews, his hearers became angry and not only threw him out of the synagogue but threatened his very life.

With the doors of the synagogue being shut to him for the time being, Jesus then went outside to do his work. He went to people where they were and called them to be his followers. True, he would be back in the synagogue again. For the time being, though, he would minister on the open road, at the market place, and by the lakeside. In today's lesson, the experiences of Jesus calling the fishermen—Peter, James, and John (plus Andrew, according to Mark 1:16–20)—and the tax collector Levi (also known as Matthew) give us insight into his call to us to follow him today.

## He Comes to Us

The experience with the fishermen took place by the Sea of Galilee. The Sea of Galilee was called by three names—the Sea of Galilee, the Sea of Tiberius, and the Lake of Gennesaret. It is thirteen miles long by eight miles wide and is 680 feet below sea level. Its climate is almost tropical. Today it is almost deserted, but in the days of Jesus, nine townships clustered around its shores, none of them with fewer than 15,000 people.

As Jesus walked along by the sea, great crowds followed him. Presently he saw the fishermen washing their nets. This was regular morning work

## Evangelism

Many ways of evangelism are taught in the Bible. We should use all of them to reach our world for Christ today. They are:

- Mass evangelism. John the Baptist and Simon Peter at Pentecost used this method. Billy Graham uses it today.
- Organized evangelism. Jesus sent out the twelve (Matthew 10:1–42), and later the seventy (Luke 10:1–17). He told them where to go, what to take, what to say, what to expect, and how to deal with rejection as they went from village to village.
- Literary evangelism. John's purpose in writing his gospel was that people might "believe that Jesus is the Christ, the Son of God; and that believing you may have life in His name" (John 20:31, NASB).
- Personal evangelism. This is one person telling another one about Christ. Everyone who studies in the field of evangelism agrees that this is by far the most effective method of evangelism. Research actually shows that most people who accept Christ are led to that conversion experience by the witness of another person, usually a friend. Personal relationships produce twice as many converts as do sermons, church services, and evangelistic events. If you look at people eyeball to eyeball and share Christ with them, they will often say "yes." Personal evangelism is every Christian's job—and joy. Will you begin now to share your faith with others?

---

for fishermen. The best fishing was done at night in deep water. With the night's work done, they were cleaning up their gear.

Jesus asked Peter to shove his boat out into the water a little way. Then, using the bow of the boat as his pulpit, Jesus spoke to the crowds. The water would make the acoustics good and thus enable the large crowd to hear his message. We are not told what Jesus said, only that he spoke to the spiritually hungry masses.

Presently, Jesus commanded Peter to take the boat out into deeper water. Jesus then told Peter to let down his nets and he'd make a big catch. Peter was an experienced fisherman; he was convinced that this was useless. They had just fished these waters all night with no luck whatsoever, and Peter, never at a loss for words, told Jesus so. There must have been a note of authority in Jesus' voice because Peter responded, "But I will do as You say and let down the nets" (Luke 5:5, NASB).

When they let down the nets, they caught so many fish that the nets literally began to break. This obvious miracle caused Simon Peter to fall at

Jesus' feet, saying, "Go away from me Lord, for I am a sinful man, O Lord!" (5:8, NASB). This should not be interpreted to mean that Peter was more sinful than others were. Rather, it means he felt the fear sinful people ought to feel in the presence of God.

Jesus then said to Peter, "Do not fear, from now on you will be catching men" (5:10, NASB). Though we can't be sure, this likely was not the first time these men had met and heard Jesus. We do know that when they had brought their boats to land another amazing thing happened. They left everything—their boats, their nets, and their lucrative business—and became Jesus' followers.

*The Lord is looking for availability and dependability, not just ability.*

Later in this chapter Jesus encountered a tax collector named Levi (Matthew) sitting in his tax office and said to him, "Follow Me" (5:27, NASB). And he, like Peter, Andrew, James, and John, "left everything behind, and got up and began to follow Him" (5:28, NASB).

The remarkable thing about this experience is that Jesus not only associated with people like Levi, but that he included them in his most intimate group of followers. Tax collectors were among the most despised people of Jesus' day. They were classified along with robbers, murderers, and harlots, and for good reason. Palestine, at that time, was occupied territory. It had been conquered by the Romans. Tax collectors served under the Roman government and therefore were regarded as renegades and traitors.

The taxation system lent itself to abuse. The Roman custom was to farm out its tax collection. Rome assessed a district a certain figure and then sold the right to collect taxes within it to the highest bidder. As long as the tax collector handed over the assessed figure at the end of the year, he was entitled to retain whatever else he could extract from the people. Too, since there was no way of making public announcements that would reach everyone, people had no idea of what they had to pay. So, the unsuspecting public was often forced to pay exorbitant taxes; they could do nothing about it. Tax collectors were so despised that the Jews barred them from the synagogues.

Levi was such a person. When he realized that Jesus was the Savior, he broke with Rome, gave up his sinful but lucrative life, and became a follower of Jesus.

## "Noticed"

The word translated "noticed" in Luke 5:27 means to "see with obvious delight." When Jesus looked at Levi, he saw beyond his sin; Jesus saw Levi's potential. At that time he was a despised man wasting his life squeezing money out of poor people. Jesus saw him not only for what he was, but also for what he might become. Jesus told him to leave his bench and his books and come and follow him. Jesus still sees the hidden potential in every person, and he calls us to follow him.

## Jesus Was an "Outsider"

Consider the idea of being an "outsider." One sense is literally to be "outside," in the open air. Life in the first century world was largely lived outside. Houses were small, air conditioning was nonexistent, and furnishings were scant. The light of the little oil lamp was poor at best. So the common people did almost everything outside except sleep. The situation is much the same in third world countries even today.

If Jesus were to reach the people of his day, he must go outside, too. In this sense, Jesus was an outsider seeking outsiders. He was actually an outsider from the first. He was born outside, literally, in a manger because there was no room for him inside. John the Baptist baptized him outside in the Jordan River. Jesus was outside when the heavens opened up and the voice thundered forth, "You are My beloved Son, in You I am well-pleased" (3:22, NASB). He was outside when he delivered history's greatest message, known as the Sermon on the Mount. He was outside when a woman crawled through the crowd to touch the hem of his garment hoping to be healed. He was outside when he fed the 5,000 with two fish and five barley loaves. He was outside when he cured blind Bartemaus. He was outside when he was transformed on the mountain and Moses and Elijah stepped across the barriers of time and came and talked with him. He was outside when he called Lazarus from the grave. Jesus was outside when he cleansed the ten lepers. He was outside when he made the supreme sacrifice by dying for us on the cross. Too, early that third day when they went to look for him on the inside of the tomb the angels said, "He is not here, but He has risen" (Luke 24:6). He was "outside."

*Only in committing ourselves to Jesus and his kingdom do we find life truly worth living.*

Consider that perhaps Jesus spent so much time outside because that's where the people were. If he had not gone outside, he'd never have reached Levi because Levi was not allowed to attend the synagogues.

Think further about this idea of being outside. If we follow Jesus we too will have to go outside—at least symbolically and perhaps even literally—because most people in Texas and in the whole of our nation are outside the church.

*People are willing to forsake all for other things. Why shouldn't we do it for Christ?*

A few years ago the once great Proctor Street Baptist Church in Port Arthur, Texas, was bought by a group of Vietnamese and turned into a Buddhist temple. The people who did this are outsiders in many senses of the word. Either they are treated as outsiders by the community, or they feel that they are outsiders. They will be reached only when we go outside the church and seek them. Like Jesus we must get "outside"—outside the church—if we're going to reach the unchurched.

## He Calls Us

Jesus' call of the fishermen and of the tax collector teaches us that Jesus not only comes to us and meets us where we are—but he calls us to be his disciples. We make a mistake if we think we must have extraordinary talents and gifts to be used by God. As far as we know, the people Jesus called from beside the lake and in the tax office were no different from other people around them. They were just ordinary people, but they had the faith to follow and obey.

The Lord is looking for availability and dependability, not just ability. We would do well to remember that the church, for the most part, has been nourished by unknown pastors and lay people who stay at it day by day and by ordinary congregations of sinners who, by grace and prodding, are being slowly cajoled into sainthood.

The call of Jesus then and now is always the same. He calls us to follow, to forsake all, and to fish. Consider his call.

First, Jesus calls us to follow. The call "follow me" is simple and easy to understand, but it implies a great deal. To follow Jesus means we have to be prepared to take the risks Jesus took. To follow Jesus means there must be no competing loyalty. Too, to follow Jesus means we must share his mission of bringing all people to God. Jesus is Lord of life, and he has every right to call us to follow and obey him. Those who hear and obey his voice are his true disciples.

There is a difference in living and just existing. Only those who commit their lives to Jesus ever experience the difference. Only in committing ourselves to Jesus and his kingdom do we find life truly worth living.

Second, Jesus calls us to forsake all. People are willing to forsake all for other things. Why shouldn't we do it for Christ?

People forsake all for medical science. Dr. Michael DeBakey of Houston, Texas, is a pioneer of cardiovascular surgery and still one of the premier heart surgeons of the world. At the age of 90 he continued to work full time, driven by the desire to solve the lingering mysteries of the human heart. DeBakey grew up in Lake Charles, Louisiana. The son of a prominent pharmacist, he had read the entire *Encyclopedia Britannica* by the time he enrolled at Tulane University. He attended college and medical school simultaneously, completing two years of medical studies by the time his bachelor's degree was in hand. DeBakey said he gave up—forsook, if you will—golf, hunting, and fishing because such pursuits took away from his true passion: medicine.

---

## Outsiders Welcome in Texas

The doormat at the ranch house of the late President Lyndon B. Johnson says, "All the world is welcome here." That has always been the spirit of Texas. Outsiders have been welcomed with open arms. If they hadn't been, there would have been no place for General Sam Houston, hero of Texas independence and first President of the Republic of Texas. He came to Texas from Tennessee. There would have been no place for James Huckins, who was the first Baptist missionary appointed to Texas. He came to Texas from New Hampshire. Or for William Tryon, who founded Baylor University. He came to Texas from New York. Or for Judge R.E.B. Baylor, who helped Tryon found Baylor. He came to Texas from Kentucky. Or for Z.N. Morrell, who preached the first Baptist sermon on Texas soil and established the first Baptist church in Texas. He came to Texas from Tennessee. Or for B.H. Carroll, who served as pastor of First Baptist Church, Waco, started the Bible department at Baylor University, and was founder and first President of Southwestern Baptist Theological Seminary. He came to Texas from Mississippi. Or for George W. Truett, famed pastor of First Baptist, Dallas, generally recognized as one of the greatest preachers Baptists have ever produced. He came to Texas from North Carolina.

Still today we welcome outsiders. Let's put that welcome mat out at our churches: "All the world is welcome here."

---

People forsake all for the arts. A concert violinist playing in New York's Carnegie Hall was asked how she became so skillful. She replied, "Planned neglect." She deliberately planned to neglect all those things that wouldn't help her to reach her goal.

People forsake all for literary fame. Nathaniel Hawthorne brooded over *The Scarlet Letter* for six years. Tennyson corrected some of his poems fifty times. Edward Gibbon spent twenty years of his life writing *The Decline and Fall of the Roman Empire.*

If people give this much effort to achieving personal goals, why then shouldn't we be willing to forsake all for Christ and his kingdom?

Third, he calls us to fish. He told Simon and the other fishermen, "From now on you will be catching men" (5:10, NASB). With that they had a new assignment in life, a new reason for being. They had a task that was worthy of their highest and best. So, Peter, Andrew, James, and John gladly left a lucrative fishing business, and Levi gladly left his profitable tax-collecting business. They all followed obediently after Jesus. The call to follow him included a break with their old way of life of fishing for fish and collecting taxes and to begin drawing people to him.

Levi is a perfect example of how quickly these men took to this new challenge. Having discovered Jesus for himself, he wished his friends to share in this great discovery. So, he gave a reception in his home with Jesus as the guest of honor. Since Levi was an outcast, all his guests would be outcasts also.

Jesus gladly accepted the invitation. Without an attitude of superiority or contempt, he mingled with Levi and his friends. The Pharisees criticized Jesus severely for doing this. Jesus, though, was not unaware of their sins and neither did he condone them. He simply knew that he must associate with people in order to deal with their sins effectively.

The Pharisees who saw Jesus doing this were filled with indignation. They wanted to know why Jesus would associate with such people. His answer was classic, "It is not those who are well who need a physician, but those who are sick. I have not come to call the righteous but sinners to repentance" (5:31–32, NASB).

Shortly after I became a Christian, my church had a weeklong study of a book by C.E. Matthews, the first Director of Evangelism for Texas Baptists. The title of the book was *Every Christian's Job*; it was a study of soul winning. So, early in my Christian life I realized that telling others about Christ was not to be left to preachers alone. It was my responsibility also.

The early church understood this, and apparently the biblical writers did not feel any necessity to urge new converts to witness. Evangelism just happened. It was the natural result of conversion and discipleship. It should be with us also.

Surveys reveal that people can be reached for Christ if we will simply reach out to them. In fact one out of every four people in America said they would attend a church if someone they knew or someone with whom they felt comfortable would invite them.

Jesus from the beginning of his ministry called people to forsake all, follow him, and become fishers of human beings. He issues that same call to us today. If we will answer Jesus' call as they did, we can make a difference in people's lives in so many ways.

## QUESTIONS

1. Have you ever felt the fire of conviction as Jesus spoke to you?

2. Where in your own experience has Jesus surprised you by coming into your situation when you least expected it?

3. Who helped you come to Christ?

4. When and where did you first hear the call of Christ?

5. Who are some of the people in your community considered as outsiders whom the church needs to reach?

6. How can the church best reach these people for Christ?

7. In what varied ways can we respond to Jesus' call and fulfill the Great Commission (Matthew 28:18–20)?

## Focal Text

Luke 7:36–50

## Background

Luke 7:36–50

## Main Focus

The person who recognizes the greatness of being forgiven responds in grateful service to God.

## Question to Explore

How do people live when they have experienced genuine forgiveness from God?

## Study Aim

To evaluate the extent of my gratitude to God for God's grace in my life

## Texas Priorities Emphasized

- Share the gospel of Jesus Christ with the people of Texas, the nation, and the world.
- Minister to human needs in the name of Jesus Christ
- Equip people for ministry in the church and in the world
- Develop Christian families
- Strengthen existing churches and start new congregations

# LESSON THREE Living as Forgiven People

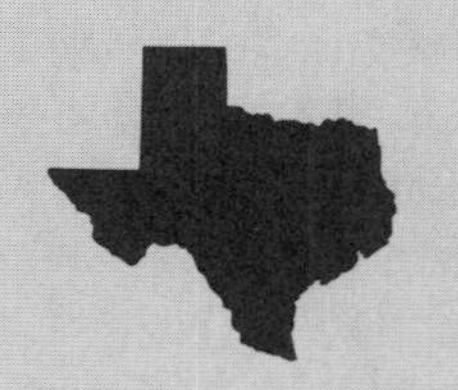

## Quick Read

When people experience God's forgiveness, they will respond in grateful service to God. Too, the greater their sense of forgiveness, the greater their loving service in return. Their service will be spontaneous, sacrificial, and shameless.

General Sam Houston was a true American giant and a Texas hero. Houston grew up in Tennessee. As a teenager, he ran away to live with the Cherokee Indians. He later joined the army and fought in the War of 1812, drawing the attention of Andrew Jackson. While serving under Jackson, Houston was wounded in the Battle of Alabama. By the time Houston was thirty-five, he was governor of Tennessee. His political career there, however, crashed when his first marriage went sour after just three months.

Houston returned to the Cherokees and took an Indian wife. While with the Cherokees, he developed such a drinking problem that the Indians gave the six-feet-six Houston the name "Big Drunk."

In 1832 Houston came to Texas and quickly became involved in politics and the brewing revolution. The fight was not against Mexico, for these people considered themselves loyal Mexican citizens. Rather the fight was against the dictator Santa Anna, who had taken away the rights of all the Mexican people that had been granted by their constitution.

Houston's place in history was secured at San Jacinto in 1836, where his outnumbered ragtag Texas army defeated Santa Anna's troops in a brief but historic battle that made Texas a republic. Houston, the General of the Army, became the President of the Republic of Texas.

Ten years later, Texas became a part of the United States. Houston served as Texas' first U.S. Senator. He held this post for thirteen years. He then was elected governor in 1859. He was deposed fifteen months later for refusing to take an oath of allegiance to the Confederacy.

Earlier, though, in May 1839, Sam Houston fell in love with Margaret Moffette Lea the first time he saw her. She was passing strawberries among the guests at a garden party in Mobile, Alabama, given by her younger sister. When Houston saw Margaret a second time later in the summer, he proposed marriage. She accepted. He was twenty-six years older than the twenty-one-year-old Margaret when they were married on May 9, 1840. Margaret, the daughter of a Baptist minister, was a devout Baptist.

Margaret was aware of Houston's habits of drinking, cursing, fighting, and womanizing. She immediately set out to accomplish his conversion. First, Houston quickly ended any adventures with or longings for any other woman; he was truly in love with Margaret. Then, she gently helped him quell his heavy drinking. It was only after fourteen years of praying and patiently waiting that she finally saw her husband baptized. Marquis James, in his remarkable Houston biography, *The Raven*, described it like this:

> Sam Houston knelt before the altar in Independence and asked to be received into the church . . . which in clerical circles assumed the scope of a national event. On the 19th of November, 1854, the convert waded the chilly waters of Rocky Creek and was baptized by Reverend Rufus C. Burleson.[1]

On October 19, 1854, Houston had gone forward at the Baptist church in Independence and said to pastor Burleson, "Today I give you my hand, and with it I give my heart to the Lord." The announcement of Houston's immersion surprised many people who thought he was past praying for. But God did a great work of grace in Sam Houston's life.

*The more we recognize the greatness of God's forgiveness, the more we want to respond with grateful service to him.*

Having been forgiven of many sins, Houston was eternally grateful to God for his mercy. The result was that immediately General Sam Houston began to pay one-half of the pastor's salary at his church and paid the tuition of scores of ministerial students at Baylor University.

Such acts of generosity and service ought always to mark the life of a forgiven person. The more we are forgiven, the more we desire to serve God out of a sense of gratitude. Houston's example is a challenge to all Texans and indeed to all believers to live as forgiven people.

The more we recognize the greatness of God's forgiveness, the more we want to respond with grateful service to him. This is the central message of our lesson today.

## Why We Serve

Many people have a mistaken view of Jesus. They think of him as an aloof, austere, and joyless person. Nothing could be further from the truth. He was an outgoing, fun-loving, people-person, who lived an active social life. He loved people, and they sensed it. As a result, he was a sought-after guest for dinners and at all kinds of festive occasions. He attended weddings (John 2:1–2). He often ate with his close friends, Mary, Martha, and Lazarus (Luke 10:38–42). He was a guest of honor at a reception given by Levi (Matthew) the tax collector (Luke 5:29). Too, on more than one occasion he ate with Pharisees (7:36; 11:37; 14:1).

Although Jesus identified primarily with people of the lower levels of society, no person or home was off limits to him. Luke 7:36–50 deals with one of those occasions when Jesus was invited to dine with a Pharisee. The Pharisee was named Simon. Jesus promptly accepted the invitation. The Pharisees were the "separated ones" of Jesus' day. They did not mix and mingle with ordinary people. Why should such a man invite Jesus to his house at all? Possibly he was an admirer of Jesus. Not all Pharisees were his enemies. Or perhaps Simon had invited Jesus to his house with the deliberate intention of enticing him or catching him in some violation of Jewish law. Perhaps he simply wanted to see and be seen with the popular young preacher. Or perhaps Simon invited Jesus out of a genuine interest to know more about what he taught and who he was.

*The one thing that shuts a person off from God is self-sufficiency.*

The scene was in the courtyard of the house of Simon. The houses of well-to-do people were built around an open courtyard in the form of a hollow square. Often in the courtyard there was a garden and a fountain. Meals were eaten in the courtyard in warm weather.

In that day, when a rabbi was at a meal in such a house, all kinds of people came in—they were quite free to do so—to listen to the pearls of wisdom that fell from his lips. This custom explains the presence of a woman of questionable character whom we shall meet in a moment.

When a guest entered a house, three things were always done. First, the host placed his hand on the guest's shoulder and gave him the kiss of peace. That mark of respect was never omitted in the case of a distinguished rabbi. Second, since the roads were only dusty tracks, and shoes

## Sam Houston's Conversion

Sam Houston's acts of generosity and service by paying one-half of his pastor's salary and supporting ministerial students attending Baylor University were not the only evidence of his genuine conversion. Shortly after he was baptized, he was riding horseback when his mount stumbled. His old nature surfaced momentarily, and he cursed the horse. According to John Reagan, with whom the general was traveling, Houston dismounted, knelt in the road, and asked for forgiveness. Houston was truly a forgiven and a converted man.

were only soles held in place by straps across the foot, always cool water was poured on the guest's feet to cleanse and comfort them. Third, either a pinch of sweet smelling incense was burned or a drop of oil containing the fragrance of roses was placed on the guest's head. These things good manners demanded, but Simon had done none of these things. This was such a breach of etiquette that Jesus could have regarded it as an insult if he had wanted to do so. Jesus did not indicate, however, that this slight bothered him.

The method of dining in the eastern world of that day was vastly different from our own. The participants did not sit in chairs at a table. They rather reclined on couches around the table, resting on their left elbow, thus leaving their right arm free. Their feet were stretched out behind them.

As the guests sat at dinner, they were surprised by the appearance of a woman who is simply identified as "a sinner" (7:37). That term carried the general connotation of ritual impurity. The woman was probably a prostitute.

No doubt the woman had listened to Jesus speak from the edge of the crowd and had glimpsed in him the hand that would lift her from the mire of her ways. Because his feet extended behind him as he reclined at the table, the woman approached Jesus unobtrusively to anoint his feet with the ointment she had brought for this purpose. Before she could carry out her mission, however, she was so overcome with emotion that she began to weep. Her tears fell on Jesus' feet. Almost immediately she stooped down and began wiping Jesus' feet with her hair and kissing them as she anointed them (7:37–38).

*It is not out of a sense of duty or obligation but out of a sense of grace and thanksgiving that we serve God.*

For a Jewish woman to appear with hair unbound was an act of grave immodesty. On her wedding day a girl bound up her hair, and never would she appear with it unbound again. The fact that this woman loosed her long hair in public showed how she had forgotten everyone but Jesus.

The woman was now doing for Jesus what Simon should have done when his guest arrived but had neglected to do so. Her gesture indicated great respect, great humility, and a sense of unworthiness in the presence of Jesus. And yet she is obviously confident that he does not have the condemning attitude of the Pharisees.

This most unusual scene disturbed Simon, the host (7:39). Knowing the character of the woman, he said to himself that if Jesus were a prophet he would have known the kind of woman who had touched him. Surely a prophet would not permit such an act by a sinful woman. A prophet would have been wise enough to reject her act as insulting. Rabbis of that day never even talked to a woman in public if they could help it. Simon concluded that Jesus either did not know the character of this woman or was lax in his attitude toward her. Simon was disturbed by the way in which Jesus accepted this respect given by such an undesirable person.

*Too many people are looking for a bargain basement religion. They want the blessings of God at a garage sale price.*

Jesus' response to Simon indicates that he not only knew the character of the woman, but he also knew the unworthy thoughts of Simon. Though Simon had not actually said a word, Jesus read his thoughts.

Turning to Simon, Jesus said, "Simon, I have something to say to you" (7:40, NASB). Then he proceeded to tell Simon a parable. It was the story of a moneylender who had two debtors. One owed 500 denarii. A Roman denarius was a silver coin that represented a day's wage for an ordinary worker. The second debtor owed only 50 denarii, one-tenth the amount of the first. Neither debtor was able to pay, and the master graciously forgave them both (7:41–42).

Jesus then asked Simon which of the two debtors would love the creditor more (7:42). Simon guessed the one who had been forgiven most, and Jesus told him he was right (7:43).

The 500 denarii represent the sins of the woman; the 50 represent the sins of Simon. Both the woman and Simon were hopelessly in debt, but Simon deluded himself into thinking that his sins were not so great by comparison to hers. The parable teaches that God is not like people, harshly demanding his pound of flesh. He freely forgave both people their debts.

Then Jesus made the application by referring to the great need of the woman and to her great service of love as compared to Simon's neglect (7:44–46). Jesus continued, telling Simon that because the woman loved much, her many sins were forgiven (7:47). Jesus then announced this fact to the woman, saying that her faith had saved her (7:48, 50).

The whole story contrasts two attitudes of mind and heart. Simon was conscious of no need. Therefore, he felt no love and received no forgiveness. Simon's impression of himself was that he was a good man in the sight of people and God. The woman was conscious of nothing else than

## The Pharisees

Two of the most influential religious parties among the Jews in Jesus' day were the Pharisees and the Sadducees. Both were political as well as religious. The very name "Pharisee" means "separatist." It indicates the nature of their emphasis.

Almost from the beginning, Jesus was in conflict with the Pharisees. Jesus and the Pharisees held vastly different concepts of religion and righteousness. In the picture the gospels paint of the Pharisees, religion for them was the sum of the laws that God had given plus the traditions handed down by the fathers who made the applications of the laws. These applications were almost more sacred than the laws themselves. On the whole the Pharisees refused to accept the new teachings of Jesus.

her need and therefore was overwhelmed with love for the One who could supply it. She received forgiveness.

The one thing that shuts a person off from God is self-sufficiency. The strange thing is that the closer to God people are, the more they feel their sin. Paul could speak of sinners "of whom I am chief" (1 Timothy 1:15, KJV). Perhaps the greatest of sins is to be conscious of none.

*We should serve God without regard for the cost. We should serve God without regard for the criticism that we might receive. We should serve God without regard for what others do or do not do.*

Simon had immediately classified the woman and dismissed her as a sinner. He had depersonalized her by thinking of her as being just like others of her ilk. But on every count the woman is shown to be Simon's superior. What she did for Jesus that day was an expression of gratitude for the acceptance and love he had shown to her. Because she knew herself to be accepted and forgiven by God, she could forgive herself and hold her head up before other people.

The miracle of Jesus' acceptance is clearly seen. As a result of Jesus' forgiveness, the prostitute discovered her own personal worth as a daughter of God. Now out of gratitude she wanted to serve the Master.

### How We Serve

Three things about this woman's act of humble service ought to challenge us today.

First, her service was spontaneous. Jesus did not demand that she do what she did anymore than he demanded that Simon provide the social amenities that were customary when he entered into Simon's house. What she did was wholly voluntary and out of a sense of deep gratitude.

Remember, there is no way we can earn our salvation. The Scriptures are clear, "For by grace you have been saved through faith; and that not of yourselves, it is the gift of God; not as a result of works, so that no one may boast. For we are His workmanship, created in Christ Jesus for good works, which God prepared beforehand so that we would walk in them" (Ephesians 2:8–10, NASB). Works cannot save. But good works always accompany salvation (see James 2:17).

Second, the woman's loving service to Christ was sacrificial. The alabaster box was a long-necked flask of fine translucent material, used for storing perfume. The box was made of beautiful and expensive stone. But the cost did not bother her. She did not count pennies when it came to serving the one who had forgiven her. Her act was gracious, generous, and unselfish.

Some people seem to know the price of everything and the value of nothing. David was once commanded to erect an altar to the Lord on the threshing floor of a man named Araunah (see 2 Samuel 24:18–25). David went to Araunah and asked to buy the threshing floor from him so that he might build an altar to the Lord. Araunah not only offered to give David the threshing floor but also to furnish the oxen that would be used in the offering. He said, "Everything, O king, Araunah gives to the king" (2 Sam. 24:23, NASB). But David would not accept his offer. He responded by saying, "No, but I will surely buy it from you for a price,

## Application

- We should never forget the greatness of God's forgiveness to us. Such forgiveness is the catalyst for greater service.
- Jesus was and is no respecter of persons. He freely fellowshiped with Pharisees and publicans alike. We would do well to put away our prejudices that keep us from relating to all people with love.
- God's grace and forgiveness are as available to the greatest sinner as to the most devout person we know.
- We should not be ashamed to show our devotion to the Lord.
- What others do or do not do should have no bearing on our service to the Lord.

for I will not offer burnt offerings to the Lord my God which cost me nothing" (2 Sam. 24:24, NASB).

Too many people are looking for a bargain basement religion. They want the blessings of God at a garage sale price. But people who are genuinely forgiven do not count the cost. They are sacrificial in their service.

Third, the woman's act was shameless. That is, she was unashamed to openly show her love and her devotion to Christ. She did not care who saw it or what they thought of it. In fact, she seemed oblivious to who might be watching or what they might be thinking.

*We serve not by comparison, but out of deep compassion and gratitude.*

The service we render to God should be like the service of this woman. We should serve God without regard for the cost. We should serve God without regard for the criticism that we might receive. We should serve God without regard for what others do or do not do. This woman might have excused her service saying, *The host did not do what he should do; so why should I?* But she would serve God regardless of what others might do.

If we are to live as forgiven people, we must be like this woman and not like the Pharisee. We must serve the Lord regardless of the cost, regardless of the criticism, and regardless of what others may do. We serve not by comparison, but out of deep compassion and gratitude.

## QUESTIONS

1. Why do you think that Luke pictures Jesus as often being at parties and dinners (see, for example, Luke 5:27–32; 7:36–38; 10:38–42; 11:37–41)?

2. What are some ways we can show our love for and gratitude to the Lord for his forgiveness?

3. What attitudes exemplified by the Pharisee are still common in the church today?

4. Who are some people in your church or among your acquaintances who show unusual love for, devotion to, and service for Christ? Do you know why they are so devoted?

5. Jesus not only knows our character, but he also knows our thoughts. Contrast the difference in the way the Pharisee thought, the way Jesus thought, and the way the woman thought.

6. What does the neglect of the Pharisee to wash Jesus' feet, greet him with the customary kiss on the cheek, and anoint his head with oil tell you about the Pharisee?

7. Recall someone who gives evidence of living as a forgiven person.

## NOTES

1. Marquis James, *The Raven: A Biography of Sam Houston* (1929; reprint, Austin: University of Texas Press, 1994), 385.

### Focal Text

Luke 10:1–17

### Background

Luke 10:1–24

### Main Focus

All Christians are sent into the world to do the Lord's work.

### Question to Explore

To what ministry is the Lord sending us, and how shall we carry it out?

### Study Aim

To identify the ministry to which the Lord is sending us and how we can carry it out

### Texas Priorities Emphasized

- Share the gospel of Jesus Christ with the people of Texas, the nation and the world
- Minister to human needs in the name of Jesus Christ
- Equip people for ministry in the church and the world
- Strengthen existing churches and start new congregations

LESSON FOUR

# Sent to Do the Lord's Work

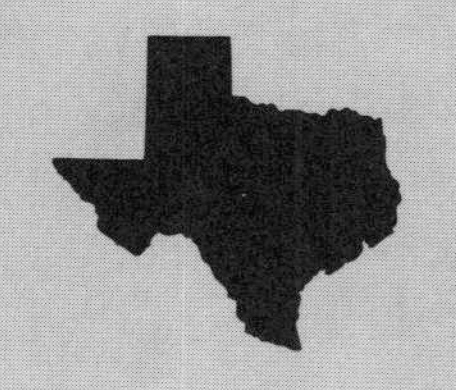

### Quick Read

The call to be a Christian is at the same time a call to be a witness. All Christians are sent into the world to do the Lord's work. His work must never be left to the professionals or a select few. Every believer—the ordinary Christian, the plain vanilla saint—is called to do the Lord's work.

In the days surrounding World War I, the United States was having trouble with German submarines. We didn't know how to deal with them. Will Rogers, the humorist, came up with a solution. He suggested all we needed to do was to boil the ocean. This would create such a pressure it would force the submarines to the top. Then we could shoot them like ducks on a pond. When someone questioned how we could boil the ocean, Will responded that he was simply telling us what to do; it was up to us to work out the details.

Often when we're discussing the work of God we speak in such broad generalities that when we get through everybody knows what to do, but nobody knows how to do it. A part of the genius of Jesus was that he not only told people what to do, but he also showed them how to do it. We find an example of this in our Scripture today. It is the account of Jesus sending out seventy disciples, two by two, to cities where he himself would come preaching shortly. Previously Jesus had sent out the twelve apostles on a similar mission (Luke 9:1–10). The sending out of the seventy indicates a rapid expansion of his preaching ministry.

The sending out of the seventy is an example of organized evangelism. A previous lesson, lesson two, indicated that four kinds of evangelism are taught in the New Testament. One is mass evangelism. The preaching of John the Baptist to great crowds and the preaching of Peter on the day of Pentecost are examples of this kind of evangelism. Another is personal evangelism. Andrew telling his brother Peter, and Philip speaking to the Ethiopian eunuch are examples of one person reaching another for Christ. Literary evangelism is a third kind. John says that his gospel was written " . . . that you may believe that Jesus is the Christ, the Son of God; and that believing you may have life in His name" (John 20:31, NASB). Organized evangelism is the fourth kind of evangelism, and this incident is an example of that kind of evangelism. Jesus told these seventy disciples where to go, what to take, how to act, what to say, and how to deal with rejection. He trained them, prepared them, and then sent them out two by two.

The number seventy was to the Jews a symbolic number. First, it was the number of the elders who were chosen to help Moses with the task of leading and directing the people in the wilderness (Numbers 11:16–25). Second, it was the number of the Sanhedrin, the supreme council of the Jews. Third, it was held to be the number of nations in the world. Luke had a world view, and it may well be that he was thinking of the day when every nation of the world would come to know and trust the Savior.

The seventy were sent out two by two after the pattern of Deuteronomy 19:15. The testimony of two people is reliable and worthy of trust. The verb "sent" indicates that these were authoritative representatives or messengers of Jesus. Their task is described as one of preparation for a subsequent mission to be undertaken by Jesus himself.

## Preparing Us for the Task

Notice in Luke 10:2 how Jesus prepared the seventy for their task. In preparing them Jesus said, "The harvest is plentiful, but the laborers are few; therefore beseech the Lord of the harvest to send out laborers into His harvest" (Luke 10:2, NASB). Jesus often used the figure of harvest to describe the ingathering of believers (Matthew 9:37–38; John 4:35). The fact and the extent of the harvest were never in question. There was only a question of workers. So the seventy were to pray that the Lord would send forth laborers.

*Things nail us to this world and can keep us from hastening on our journey to bring people to heaven.*

Then, in Luke 10:2–11, Jesus gave them specific instructions for their journey and their ministry. They were to go courageously. They would be as lambs in the midst of wolves (10:3). As Jesus was in the world unarmed and exposed to rejection, so they would be in the world. It would take a special courage to accomplish their mission.

Verse 4 indicates that they were to go in faith. They were to travel completely divested of provisions. They were not to take a moneybag or other provisions. Their lives were not to be cluttered with material things. They were to travel light. It is easy to get entangled and enmeshed in material things. Things nail us to this world and can keep us from hastening on our journey to bring people to heaven. They were to trust God to provide for their needs.

Too, they were to go with a sense of urgency. They were to "greet no one on the way" (10:4, NASB). This does not mean that they were to be unfriendly. Rather it means that they were not to be delayed or embarrassed by the tedious and often meddlesome oriental salutations. They must not turn aside or linger on the lesser things while the great things called them.

Also, they were to be congenial as they entered a home. The greeting they were to use was the ancient Semitic *shalom* or peace, which was basically a wish for the other person's well being. The greeting as Jesus used it in verse 5 stands for the peace of God, which we can possess now if we trust in the Messiah.

In addition, the seventy were to go with gratitude and acceptance. Their assignment would require hospitality from others (see 10:6–7). If people welcomed them into their home, they were to accept the invitation and eat whatever was placed before them. They were to be messengers, not beggars. Moreover, they were not to wander from house to house looking for more comfortable quarters and more congenial company. Their preoccupation was to be with their mission, not with the

## Our Accountability

This teaching of Jesus brings us face to face with our accountability to God. What things will be considered in the judgment? What factors will be taken into account?

- We will be judged by the law of God written in our hearts. All people have an awareness of God, and all people have a knowledge of right and wrong (Romans 2:15–16). Therefore, we are without excuse (1:20; 2:1).
- We will be judged by our knowledge. If we know our Lord's will and we do not do it, we shall be punished severely. If we do not know his will though we are equally disobedient, we shall receive leniency (Luke 12:48).
- We will be judged by our opportunities. It will be more tolerable in the judgment for people who have never had an opportunity to respond to Christ than for those who have had an opportunity and willfully rejected him (Matthew 11:21–22; Luke 10:14; 2 Peter 2:21).
- We will be judged by our words. We shall give an account for every idle word (Matthew 12:36–37).
- We will be judged as we have judged others. The same standards and criteria we use in criticizing and condemning others will be used by the Lord to judge us (Matthew 7:1–2).
- We will be judged by our acts of kindness and generosity. Even "a cup of water" given in Christ's name will not go unnoticed and unrewarded (Matthew 10:42; 25:31–46; Hebrews 6:10).

In short, our judgment will be related to our total life. The very fact that there are so many factors that will be taken into account in the judgment means that we will not all be judged the same and that there will be degrees of both rewards and punishment in eternity.

quality of their hospitality. Note that they were not to have a sense of guilt about living on the generosity of others. Those who bear the message of the kingdom of God are worthy of being supported by its recipients (1 Cor. 9:4–11). The laborer is worthy of his hire, but the servant of the crucified master must not be a seeker of luxury. Note, too, that evidently they were relieved of the burdens and restrictions imposed by Jewish food laws. They must eat whatever is set before them.

*"I want to warn you, once you see the poverty and darkness that is in this place, you are just as responsible as I am to do something about it. Now, do you still want to go?"*

Furthermore, they were to go with clarity of purpose. They were to say to people, "The kingdom of God has come near to you" (Luke 10:9, NASB). The kingdom of God was present in the world in the person of Jesus Christ. These were his authorized representatives, and people could enter into God's kingdom by receiving their message.

The missionaries were to go out with the word of salvation. If the hearers did not receive the message, these disciples were to "wipe the dust" from their feet and move on (10:11). Perhaps for the encouragement of the seventy, Jesus prepared them for rejection of their message by certain cities. They were to understand that they were identified with Christ and that for people to reject his messengers was the same as rejecting him.

Then the Master pronounced woes of judgment on three highly favored cities, Chorazin, Bethsaida, and Capernaum (see 10:13–15). First he pronounced his judgment on Chorazin and Bethsaida. He said it would be more tolerable on the day of judgment for Sodom, Tyre, and Sidon than it would be for these cities.

Sodom was noted as one of the most wicked cities that ever existed. Its fate of being destroyed by fire and brimstone was a historical fact well known by the Jews (see Genesis 19:1–29).

Tyre and Sidon were Gentile cities, Phoenician ports, and were looked upon as centers of idolatry and evil. If these cities had seen the miracles and heard the message that the cities to which Jesus had preached had seen and heard, they would have repented long before and put on sackcloth and ashes (Luke 10:12–15). Sackcloth, which was coarse material made of goat's or camel's hair, was worn as a symbol of great mourning over sins.

Jesus pronounced his concluding woe on Capernaum, which was the home of his most faithful disciples (see 4:31, 38), headquarters of his

Galilean ministry, and scene of many of his mighty works. The mighty works Jesus spoke about included healing the sick, cleansing lepers, and raising the dead. His mighty acts had no effect on Capernaum. Instead the arrogant city had self-righteously rejected Jesus' message and refused to humble itself in repentance.

Verse 16 indicates that the disciples were Jesus' personal delegates and to hear them was to hear Jesus. To reject them was to reject Jesus.

It is not for us to say how tolerable it will be for any in the judgment, but Jesus made it clear that the degree of tolerableness will depend on opportunities and their use. Such a principle does not promise a very comfortable position for modern cities in our nation and state.

## Knowledge Brings Responsibility

To reject God's invitation is a terrible thing. Those who hear the word of God have great responsibility. They will be judged according to what they have had a chance to know. We allow things in a child we condemn in an adult; we forgive things in a savage we would punish in a civilized person. Responsibility is the other side of privilege.

This truth was brought home to me years ago when I traveled to Mexico with two men from my church to survey a mission situation. Missionary Robert Smith told us of a town of 15,000 people that had no church at all. It had for years been the center for drug smuggling along the Texas-Mexico border. He tried as best he could to prepare us for the poverty and spiritual darkness we would encounter when we got there. Just before we reached the international bridge that crossed into Mexico, he pulled the car off on the shoulder of the highway and said, "I want to warn you, once you see the poverty and darkness that is in this place, you are just as responsible as I am to do something about it. Now, do you still want to go?"

*Success is temporary and passing. Our relationship to God is permanent and abiding. We are to find our lasting joy in the fact that our names are written in the Lamb's book of life.*

His words stung me and frightened me, for I knew that knowledge always brings with it a corresponding responsibility. As Jesus said on another occasion, "From everyone who has been given much, much will be required; and to whom they entrusted much, of him they will ask all the more" (12:48, NASB).

## "Send"

The word "send" used by Jesus in his statement, "Therefore beseech the Lord of harvest to send out laborers into His harvest" (Luke 10:2, NASB), is a very strong word. It literally means to hurl, to cast, to throw violently. It is a word used elsewhere in the Bible to describe Jesus casting demons out of people (Mark 7:26).

Jesus is here urging us to pray that there shall come such an irresistible compulsion on the hearts of men and women, boys and girls, that they cannot help but witness and work for him.

When the seventy returned from their missionary journeys, they were filled with joy saying, "Lord, even the demons are subject to us in Your name" (10:17, NASB). These disciples no longer needed to live in constant fear of the evil powers. The demons were subject to them as the representatives of Christ.

At the same time Jesus cautioned them that they were not to rejoice in the fact that the demons were subject to them but rather that their names were recorded in heaven (10:20). What did he mean by this? He was warning them not to rejoice in their success. Rather, they were to rejoice in their relationship with God. Success is temporary and passing. Our relationship to God is permanent and abiding. We are to find our lasting joy in the fact that our names are written in the Lamb's book of life.

*In far too many instances the gathering in of the harvest, the work of evangelism, has been relegated to the professional ministry when in reality it belongs to the whole church.*

### The Challenge to Us

This Scripture passage contains several messages for us. First, the great need of the world is for laborers. The fields are ripe unto harvest, but we are suffering from a labor shortage. In far too many instances the gathering in of the harvest, the work of evangelism, has been relegated to the professional ministry when in reality it belongs to the whole church. Most ministers are both overworked and underemployed. They are overworked with a thousand little things and underemployed at the most essential thing—carrying the good news of Jesus Christ to all people everywhere. If the work is to be done effectively, it must be done by laypeople—by ordinary Christians.

Second, if we are to meet the pressing needs of our state, we must begin with prayer. Jesus said to his disciples, "Therefore beseech the Lord of harvest to send forth laborers out into His harvest" (10:2, NASB). For Jesus, prayer was not a last resort; it was a first inclination. He did not urge them to begin by organizing an outreach effort or even by teaching a course of evangelism. He encouraged them to begin by praying that God would raise up a vast laboring crew to gather in the harvest.

*For Jesus, prayer was not a last resort; it was a first inclination.*

Third, we must get out of the church and into the world where people are. Today we have projected the idea that the church is a group of people streaming to a shrine to make up an audience for a speaker. The church can never be a group of people sitting in a sanctuary listening to a speaker. The church must ever be a laboring crew engaged in gathering in a harvest.

Significantly, at the very time Jesus said the fields were ripe but the laborers were few, many priests and Levites were working at the Temple. But while they kept the worship and the work of the Temple going, the world was perishing. Jesus did not go to the Temple and wait for people to come to him. Rather he trained, organized, and commissioned his disciples to go where the people were.

I was once encouraging the people of my congregation to share the gospel with their circle of friends. The chairman of the deacons said to me, "Preacher, I don't have any lost people in my circle of friends." I said to him, "Then you're spending too much time in church." We can't spend all of our time in the church house and win our world to Christ. We must mix and mingle with the lost, develop friendships with them, and out of those relationships share the good news of the kingdom of God.

*We must get out of the church and into the world where people are.*

Many churches remind me of the man whose neighbor had an oil well. He noticed the oil well pumping day in and day out, week in and week out, year in and year out. But he also noticed that his neighbor never sold any oil. One day he got up enough courage to ask the man why. The man said, "It takes all the oil we produce just to keep the machinery going." Often in our churches it takes all of our energy and effort just to keep the organization, the machinery, going. By the time we get that done, we have no energy or inclination left to go out into the world and gather in the harvest.

The fields are ripe but the laborers are few. We must do the work of God because the night is coming when no one shall work (John 9:4). We must hurry before sundown!

Finally, we can go in confidence knowing that if we share the message, we have the authority of Christ with us. Some will believe and be saved, and the population of heaven will be increased. That, after all, is the great mission of the church.

## QUESTIONS

1. In what way can we tell that the fields are ripe unto harvest around us?

2. What is the greatest need of your church in relationship to its central mission?

3. What is some difficult experience, some rejection or resistance, that you have encountered while trying to witness for Christ?

4. When, where, and how did you come to Christ?

5. Is there some need you know about and that the Lord will hold you accountable for meeting?

6. What are the qualities needed to be an effective witness today?

7. If you do not know of any lost people, where can you begin with the harvest?

8. In order to evangelize Texas, early ministers and missionaries rode horseback, swam swollen rivers, braved Texas' "blue northers," preached to people wherever they could find them, and often died prematurely as they sought to win people to Christ and organize converts into cooperating Baptist churches. What can we do to repay our debt of gratitude to them?

# The Baptist World Alliance

Founded in 1905, the Baptist World Alliance is an organization of Baptists from throughout the world to promote fellowship, evangelism, ethics, and ministry among Baptists. Membership is voluntary, and the Alliance assumes no authority over member bodies.

Baptists from 23 nations attended the first meeting of the Alliance. Every five years the Alliance sponsors a "congress," a gathering of persons from all of the Baptist entities related to the Alliance. The marvelous growth of Baptist work worldwide is seen in the fact that at the congress in 1995, 188 Baptist bodies were represented. The congress in 2000 is scheduled for Melbourne, Australia.

The Baptist World Alliance functions with a small employed staff and a large number of elected officers and volunteers. Most visible among these are the president of the Alliance and the general secretary. The president is elected at each congress and serves for five years until the next congress. George W. Truett, the world famous Texas Baptist pastor, served as president of the Alliance in the 1930s. Numerous Texas Baptists have served and currently serve in various offices and on a variety of committees and commissions of the Alliance. The general secretary not only supervises the staff, located in McLean, Virginia, but also travels extensively to speak in Baptist meetings throughout the world and encourage Baptist work.

The Alliance also functions through a General Council made up of elected representatives from the various member bodies. The Council meets each year in a different part of the world. Other organizations of the Alliance include the Women's Department, the Men's Department, and the Youth Department as well as divisions for communication, evangelism, education, study, and research. The Youth Department sponsors periodic large gatherings of Baptist youth from throughout the world in congresses, the last one being held in Houston, Texas. Special commissions, on which Texas Baptists are represented, focus on particular issues, such as racism.

A significant aspect of the Alliance's ministry is Baptist World Aid. In cooperation with member bodies, Baptist World Aid provides goods, services, and funds for persons in need throughout the world. The Baptist

General Convention of Texas assists with these efforts through the annual World Hunger Offering.

Through the years, Texas Baptists have participated in the Baptist World Alliance, and currently that involvement is increasing.

—WILLIAM M. PINSON, JR.

UNIT

# Loving Every Person

Jesus was a people person. He came to earth from the Father to reveal God's love for all people. His death on the cross was God's ultimate act of love for all of us. Too, Jesus demonstrated through his life and ministry how we should love every person, without distinction. These lessons from Luke's Gospel present us with situations from Jesus' ministry where he emphasized the importance of loving all people and especially those who, for whatever reason, may appear to be unlovable.

From lesson five we can learn to help a hurting stranger. Lesson six brings out the truth that people needs take precedence over rules and traditions. Lesson seven emphasizes the resurrection of Jesus and especially our responsibility to share the message of the risen Christ with all people everywhere.[1] Lesson eight challenges us to reconsider who we really receive and accept into our fellowship. How and whether we celebrate the salvation of others is the question of lesson nine. Altogether, these five lessons have the potential to revolutionize the way we think and act toward others, and especially those we may have ignored or neglected.

The good news is that Texas Baptists are determined to follow Jesus' model in loving and serving people. Our stated priorities include equipping people to share God's truth in love with every person and to minister to human needs wherever they are found. The challenge before us as individuals and churches is to translate our priorities into action.

---

1. When lesson seven does not coincide with Easter, it can be studied either at this point or at the end of the study.

## Focal Text

Luke 10:25–37

## Background

Luke 10:25–37

## Main Focus

We are to love every person Jesus loves and to go out of our way to demonstrate that love.

## Question to Explore

How do loving people really act?

## Study Aim

To define love as Jesus does and decide on ways I will practice that kind of love

## Texas Priorities Emphasized

- Share the gospel of Jesus Christ with the people of Texas, the nation and the world
- Minister to human needs in the name of Jesus Christ
- Equip people for ministry in the church and in the world

# LESSON FIVE What's the Least I Can Do?

## Quick Read

When we love people the Jesus way, we will be sensitive to their needs and will act in specific ways to relieve their pain.

Bill Gravell is an evangelist. He is a former student of the Baptist university where I teach. Bill recently returned to our campus to speak in a chapel service. His message was based on Luke 10:25–37, Jesus' parable of the Good Samaritan. The title of Bill's message was, "Get Off Your Donkey." He challenged us to help helpless people.

Three men passed a person hurting and helpless by the side of the road. Only one got off his donkey to help. Texas Baptists, we need to get off our donkeys.

## Loving People Begins with Loving God (10:25–28)

Jesus' ministry attracted both admirers and detractors. In the incident in Luke 10:25–37, he was within six months of the cross. The crowds were not as large and enthusiastic as before. His critics continued to build their case against him. They looked for opportunities to take issue with him. His attitude toward their understanding and interpretation of the law was under constant scrutiny. Jesus had made it clear from the beginning that he had not come to set aside the law but to fulfill it (Matthew 5: 17). The Scribes and Pharisees, however, did not trust him. They would not miss an opportunity to discredit him.

The "expert in the law" referred to in Luke 10:25 (NIV) was representative of Jesus' critics. Jesus was teaching. The law expert bristled at something he said. The law expert rose to his feet to interrupt and challenge Jesus. His intent was to test him, to trip him up, to upstage Jesus in the presence of others. "What must I do to inherit eternal life?" he queried (10:25, NIV). The question would have been the subject of discussion and debate in settings where teachers and experts in the law got together. The question got to the heart of what both the law and the teaching of Jesus were about. How can a person be right with God in the here and the hereafter? It was not unlike a question the Philippian jailer later addressed to the Apostle Paul: "What must I do to be saved?" (Acts 16:30, NIV).

The questioner was well qualified to pursue the subject he had addressed. Not a lawyer in the sense we think of today, he was expert in the law of God as it had been delivered to Moses. He would know how the law had been interpreted and expanded into what is commonly called the tradition. He was not asking Jesus for information. Apparently he asked with the anticipation that Jesus might say something incorrect or in some way disagree with his foregone conclusions. He was looking for an opening to embarrass Jesus and to silence him.

Jesus, always unpredictable in how he handled such inquiries, responded, not with an answer but with a question. "'What is written in the Law?' he replied.'How do you read it?'" (10:26, NIV). As he asked the question, Jesus may have gestured toward a phylactery positioned at the center of the law expert's forehead. That would be a small cylindrical box containing the essence of the law, worn to declare one's piety and orthodoxy. Inside the box written on bits of parchment would be the words of Deuteronomy 6:4–5, the *Shema*, Israel's confession of faith in God, and also Leviticus 19:18, which called for loving your neighbor. Displaying one's religious belief in this way would be in keeping with Deuteronomy 6:6–8.

The law expert answered with confidence: "'Love the Lord your God with all your heart and with all your soul and with all your strength and with all your mind'; and, 'Love your neighbor as yourself'" (Luke 10:27, NIV). Without hesitating, Jesus responded: "You have answered correctly. . . . Do this and you will live" (10:28, NIV). The law expert was surely disappointed that Jesus so readily agreed with him. Not willing to let the matter rest, he asked a second question.

---

## Samaritans

The Samaritans of the New Testament era were the offspring of marriages between Jews and Gentiles. They lived in the central part of Israel, west of the Jordan. The territory known as Samaria lay between Galilee on the north and Judea on the South. The Assyrians conquered the Northern Kingdom of Israel in 722 B.C. and transported most of the residents to other conquered lands. The Israelites left behind intermarried with other conquered people who were relocated to their homeland. Hence, the Samaritans were of mixed parentage.

When the Jews of the Southern Kingdom returned from Babylonian captivity about 535 B.C., they started to rebuild the Temple in Jerusalem. They refused Samaritan help. The result was a wound that would not heal. Hostility between the two people groups increased so that by Jesus' time, Jews avoided all contact with Samaritans, refusing to enter their houses or even to pass through their land.

Jesus challenged this blatant prejudice. His dealings with and references to Samaritans became opportunities to emphasize the worth of all people in God's sight.

---

Before we address that question, is it possible we are not completely comfortable with Jesus' answer? Do we expect something more traditional from a Christian perspective, something we may have learned as a part of our training for sharing the gospel, something that specifies believing in and receiving Jesus as our personal Savior? That is understandable, for we affirm the centrality of atonement through Jesus Christ as the way of salvation. Be aware, though, that this incident was before Jesus' death and resurrection. This was a proper answer to the law expert's question. Jesus affirmed what the law expert said without qualification.

*This parable provides us with a model of loving service. It talks to us about the least we can do if we truly are to be followers of Jesus.*

Jesus on another occasion (Matt. 22: 35–40; Mark 12: 28–31) in responding to a question "Which is the greatest commandment in the law?" (Matt. 22:36, NIV) answered as did this law expert. Love for God with all your heart, soul, strength and mind means loving him with your whole being, loving him from the inside out. To love God in this way means to give your whole self to him mentally, emotionally, and physically. This lesson focuses on loving your neighbor, but loving people begins with loving God. The great commandment to love God and neighbor is really one commandment in two parts. Jesus taught that to keep this commandment is to have eternal life.

## Loving People Means Being Sensitive to Their Needs (10:29–33)

Luke 10:29 indicates that the law expert evidently had hoped for a better outcome. Jesus had turned the tables on him. It would have been better for him at this point to leave well enough alone and acknowledge the wisdom of Jesus. Instead, the law expert wanted to justify himself. He needed to save face. "And who is my neighbor?" he asked (10:29, NIV). Love for God is not a matter up for debate, and so the red-faced law expert sought a refinement of the second part of the commandment.

We are not surprised that he asked this for there had been continuing discussion and disagreement about the identity of one's neighbor. Surely, the scribes reasoned, it did not refer to one's enemies. They had concluded that one should love his neighbors but hate his enemies. Jesus challenged that in the Sermon on the Mount, saying: "You have heard that it was said, 'Love your neighbor and hate your enemy.' But I tell you: Love your enemies and pray for those who persecute you, that you may be sons of your Father in heaven" (Matt. 5: 43–45, NIV). Once the definition of neighbor was limited, it was easier to subtract people like tax collectors, Samaritans, and other undesirables. So what do you say, Jesus, about who we are responsible to love?

Jesus declined to give an abstract answer. He could have said "anyone and everyone." Instead he told a story so vivid and profound it would never be forgotten.

Jesus began, "A man was going down from Jerusalem to Jericho" (Luke 10:30, NIV). Everyone knew that treacherous stretch of road. It snaked its way through rugged mountains where boulders and caves provided cover for men bent on robbery and violence. The road descended for just over twenty miles from the heights of Jerusalem at 2300 feet above sea level to Jericho just under 1300 feet below sea level. People frequented that road both coming and going, but to travel it alone would be taking a risk. The man in Jesus' story was exposing himself to danger.

Robbers accosted the man. They took everything he had, even stripping off his clothes. They mercilessly beat him and left him bruised, bloody, and near death. His naked body was exposed to the sun and wind, to wild animals and birds of prey. How could he possibly survive?

*Anyone who needs me is my neighbor.*

A priest happened by. This descendant of Aaron may well have been departing Jerusalem after performing religious services at the Temple. There he would have been involved in the offering of sacrifices or performing other Temple rituals. He was a member of the clergy as we would understand it today. He was informed in matters of the law. The command to love your neighbor was well known to him. The priest saw the body of the victim of cruelty at the side of the road. He ignored him. He chose to continue his journey, taking the other side of the road.

Next came a Levite. The Levites were by ancient authority dedicated to religious service. They assisted the priests and performed the more mundane tasks of Temple upkeep. Like the priest, he would have been versed in the essentials of Mosaic law. He also ignored the plight of the desperate dying man and chose the far side of the road, lest he become more exposed to the victim's pain.

The best way to speculate about why the priest and Levite refused help in a situation that cried for their attention is to put ourselves in their place.

Were we passing that way we might have reasoned: "I don't want to get involved. I just don't have time for this. The man should have known better than to put himself in harm's way. Someone will come along better equipped to help him."

If their hearts were at all moved with compassion, they repressed those feelings. They refused to be sensitive to the needs of a fellow human. They did not think of him as one of the neighbors they were commanded to love.

Was the man then to die by the side of the road because no one cared? No! A Samaritan travelling that way saw him and had compassion for him. Yes, a Samaritan, an outsider, a half-breed, was the hero of the parable. He saw the need and responded. His concern for a suffering man would not allow him to do nothing. Surely he was as busy as the others were. This would take valuable time from his journey. He would be involved in another person's problems. For now, however, the needs of this abused stranger became his first priority.

## Loving People Calls for Acting to Meet Their Needs (10:34–37)

"He took pity on him" (10:33, NIV). The Samaritan felt for the wounded traveler. Pity is an emotional reaction, the way we feel when we see hungry children on TV. Pity is that knot that forms in the pit of the stomach when we hear someone has lost her job or has been diagnosed with cancer. Pity is the grief we share with others when a family member dies. Pity, however, is worthless unless it translates into action. We can feel badly for people and never do anything to help them. What is important is for us to act to relieve suffering, to minister to people. W. Oscar Thompson, Jr. in his insightful book, *Concentric Circles of Concern,* defines

## Application Actions

- Identify a person to whom you can be a Good Samaritan this week.
- Make certain your Sunday School class puts God's Word to work in ministering to people's needs.
- Get involved in your church's ministry to the poor. If there is no such ministry, use your influence to get one started.
- Find a way to minister to people through an agency or institution in your community such as a hospital, a nursing home, or a jail.

love as meeting people's needs.[1] The hero of Jesus' parable can correctly be called "The Good Samaritan," because he took care of the hurting man's needs.

The Samaritan got off his donkey and approached the man. He touched him. He took out his first century first-aid kit, which included appropriate bandaging material and medicines. He dressed the wounds as best he could by the side of the road. The oil and wine were used to soothe and heal. Then he helped the man onto the back of his donkey. Picture the Samaritan holding the man in place as he walked alongside the donkey to the nearest inn. There, in more favorable surroundings, he continued to minister to the badly bruised man. He stayed with him through the night and paid his bill before leaving the next day. Still he was not through, not ready to assume someone else would take over. "Look after him . . . and when I return, I will reimburse you for any extra expense you may have," he said to the innkeeper (10:35, NIV). This Samaritan caregiver would not accept closure of the matter until he was sure he had done all he could.

*Being a neighbor means doing whatever we can to meet a person's need.*

Now comes the defining moment of this conversation between Jesus and the law expert. "Which of these three do you think was a neighbor to the man who fell into the hands of robbers?" Jesus asked (10:36, NIV). Pressed to give the only possible answer, realizing he was not going to be able to justify himself, the law expert meekly answered: "The one who had mercy on him" (10:37, NIV). Did he purposely refuse to say "the Samaritan," which would have been the more natural answer? "Go and do likewise," Jesus charged, ending the conversation (10:37, NIV).

Does the parable answer the question, "Who is my neighbor?" It does that and more. In one sense, it leaves the impression that anyone who needs me is my neighbor. At another level, it says defining who is my neighbor is not as important as being a neighbor. The challenge to the law expert and to us is to be neighbors to those who are in need. Being a neighbor means doing whatever we can to meet a person's need.

## Get Off Your Donkey!

The emphasis is on "do" in verse 37. Earlier in the conversation Jesus had implied that loving God calls for doing (10:28). How can we love God except by doing what God requires? Jesus said, "If you love me, you will obey what I command" (John 14:15, NIV). "Anyone who does not do what is right is not a child of God; nor is anyone who does not love his brother" (1 John 3: 10, NIV). "Those who obey his commands live in him, and he in them" (1 John 3:24, NIV).

*We must go and do in Jesus' name.*

The word "do" in Luke 10:37 applies to loving your neighbor. Love without deeds is like faith without works. "What good is it, my brothers, if a man claims to have faith but has no deeds? Can such faith save him? Suppose a brother or sister is without clothes and daily food. If one of you says to him, 'Go, I wish you well; keep warm and well fed,' but does nothing about his physical needs, what good is it?" (James 2:14–16, NIV). "If anyone has material possessions and sees his brother in need but has no pity on him, how can the love of God be in him?" (1 John 3:17, NIV)

*We can feel badly for people and never do anything to help them. What is important is for us to act to relieve suffering, to minister to people.*

One of our Texas Baptist priorities is to minister to human needs in the name of Jesus Christ. This parable provides us with a model of loving service. It talks to us about the least we can do if we truly are to be followers of Jesus.

There are many hungry, hurting, and homeless people in our communities. One on one spontaneous acts of service such as that described in the parable are needed. Cooperative efforts through the church are desirable. We can be involved in community programs. We can exercise our vote and influence in favor of people-centered persons and programs. We must go and do in Jesus' name. Get off your donkey.

## QUESTIONS

1. How could the priest and Levite justify ignoring a hurting person?

2. What motivated the Samaritan to stop and help when others did not?

3. Why do you think Jesus made a Samaritan the hero of this parable?

4. Would you stop to help in a comparable situation? Why? Why not?

5. Who in your class or church is most like the Good Samaritan?

## NOTES

1. W. Oscar Thompson, Jr., *Concentric Circles of Concern* (Nashville, Tennessee: Broadman Press, 1981), 84

## Focal Text

Luke 13:10–17

## Background

Luke 6:6–11; 13:10–17; 14:1–6

## Main Focus

Helping people in need takes precedence over keeping rules.

## Question to Explore

What rules keep us from ministering to people as Jesus would?

## Study Aim

To identify ways we may be letting rules, customs, or traditions keep us from ministering to people as Jesus would

## Texas Priorities Emphasized

- Share the gospel of Jesus Christ with the people of Texas, the nation and the world
- Minister to human needs in the name of Jesus Christ
- Equip people for ministry in the church and in the world

LESSON SIX

# What's More Important—Rules or People?

## Quick Read

God is glorified when ministering to people in need takes precedence over rules and traditions.

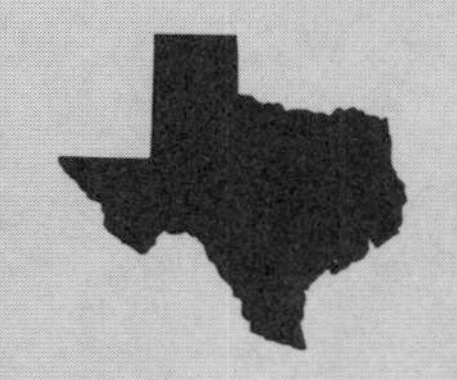

Pat M. Neff was the governor of Texas. Later he was president of Baylor University. Neff complained that preachers were always telling him to lay up treasures in heaven, but they never told him how. Finally, he realized the way to invest in heaven was to invest in what was going there and that would be people.

Texas Baptist priorities emphasize reaching and ministering to people. When we do that, we are making an investment of eternal significance. We are in the people business. We Texas Baptists must not get bogged down in rules and traditions. We must continue to ask, "What would Jesus do?" The answer is clear: Jesus would put people first. What counts is what we do for people in Jesus' name.

## Ministry to People Is a Priority (13:10–13)

Jesus grew up in a devout family. Joseph, the carpenter of Nazareth, was a godly man. He obeyed the law and adhered to the traditions of his Jewish heritage. Mary had surrendered her life to do God's will and, while still a virgin, gave birth to Jesus. Much of the life of such a family would have revolved around the local synagogue.

The synagogue had emerged as a place of worship during the Babylonian captivity of the sixth century B.C. The Temple had been destroyed, and the Jews of that time found themselves in a new environment that called for changes in the way they worshipped and served God. When the Jews returned from captivity and rebuilt the Temple, they continued to focus on synagogue worship. By Jesus' time synagogues were everywhere. They served as schools and community centers but especially for worship on the Sabbath. Here the Old Testament Scriptures were read and taught, and prayers were offered to God.

Luke makes it clear that attendance at Sabbath day services in the synagogues was a regular habit with Jesus (4:16). Jesus often taught in the synagogues, reading and explaining the Scriptures. Early in his ministry at his hometown synagogue in Nazareth, Jesus had read from Isaiah 61:1–2 and announced he was the fulfillment of that well-known messianic prophecy. He had been well received, even praised, to that point, but then the attitude changed. The people ushered him out to the brow of the hill at the edge of town. They were prepared to throw him down the cliff, but he made his way through the crowd and went on his way (Luke 4:28–30).

The Sabbath day was among the most revered of the institutions of Judaism. After creating the heavens and the earth in six days, God rested on the seventh day and set it apart as holy (Genesis 2: 2–3). "Remember the Sabbath day by keeping it holy" (Exodus 20:8, NIV) is the fourth of the Ten Commandments. Obviously, Jesus kept the Sabbath as it was intended. He broke with the religious establishment of the time, however, when he rejected the severe limitations they had placed on Sabbath observance. The teachers of the law had added rule after rule to the original commandment. They had interpreted and expanded the prohibition against work to the point it had become burdensome to the people.

*We must continue to ask, "What would Jesus do?"*

A man Jesus healed on the Sabbath was rebuked for carrying his mat, no more than a primitive bed roll on which he had lain helpless for thirty-eight years (John 5:1–14). Another time the disciples of Jesus were criticized for harvesting grain when passing through a farmer's field, though they gathered just enough to satisfy their hunger (Luke 6:1–5). When Jesus healed people on the Sabbath, as he did on several occasions in the Gospels, he was accused of breaking the law. His detractors could not understand why Jesus went against long-standing traditions. In truth he was challenging them to rise above legalism and honor God by putting aside the human rules that got in the way of helping people in need.

The Scripture text for today finds Jesus teaching in the synagogue on the Sabbath. A severely handicapped woman was there. Perhaps she struggled in during the middle of the service. She was doubled over and could not straighten up. She had suffered with this condition for eighteen years. Luke, a physician, indicates the crippling was from a demonic spirit. He recognized that in some cases there is a direct connection between physical and spiritual problems.

When Jesus saw her, he stopped in the middle of his teaching and called her forward. He said to her, "Woman, you are set free from your infirmity" (13:12, NIV). He put his hands on her, and she straightened up, giving praise to God. This action by Jesus clearly shows he was more concerned for people than for rules and traditions.

When Jesus' disciples were charged with breaking the law for plucking grain to eat on the Sabbath, he made his most important pronouncement concerning the Holy Day: "The Sabbath was made for man, not man for the Sabbath. So the Son of Man is Lord even of the Sabbath" (Mark 2:27–28, NIV). God's first concern is for people. People are more important than religious rules and institutions. God did not make a special day and then people to conform to it; God made people and then gave them a day for physical and spiritual renewal. People were not made for the church; the church was made for people.

*Could one reason new churches often grow faster than older ones be because they do not have a backlog of tradition to maintain? They can be more sensitive to what ministers to people.*

On another occasion Jesus was teaching in a synagogue where a man with a shriveled hand was present (Luke 6:6–11). The Pharisees and teachers of the law were watching what he would do, looking for grounds to accuse him. Jesus challenged them: "I ask you, which is lawful on the Sabbath: to do good or to do evil, to save life or to destroy it?" (6:9, NIV). He responded to their deafening silence by healing the man's hand. Jesus clearly endorsed ministry to the needs of people on any and every day, including the Sabbath.

## Rules and Traditions Can Hinder Ministry to People (13:14–16)

Other than his claim to a special relationship to God, Jesus' most serious conflict with the religious leadership of his day concerned their legalistic interpretations of God's Word and will. A law-bound theology inevitably diminishes the importance of people. Rules can become idols that stand between a person and his or her relationship to God. Furthermore, rules often handicap our ministry to people.

*This action by Jesus clearly shows he was more concerned for people than for rules and traditions.*

The synagogue ruler in the passage before us was beside himself with anger at what Jesus did for this woman. You would think this man, a religious leader in the community, would have rejoiced at the dramatic healing of a woman whom he more than likely knew, who had been suffering for eighteen years. Instead, he berated the congregation, saying, "There are six days for work. So come and be healed on those days, not on the Sabbath" (13:14, NIV). Does anyone think such a man would have been an instrument in this woman's healing on any day of the week? It is apparent the ruler's outrage was

## Hypocrisy

The background of the word *hypocrite* is in the Greek theatre. Literally a hypocrite is an actor, one who plays a part or role. An actor might wear a mask to hide his true identity. Men would dress like women to do a feminine part. In that setting the word hypocrite was somewhat neutral, but in the New Testament it has a negative connotation. It suggests pretense or duplicity.

Hypocrites pretend to be something they are not. In the Sermon on the Mount, Jesus denounced those who practiced their religion, whether in giving, praying, or fasting, to be seen by others (Matthew 6:1–18).

Jesus called the Pharisees hypocrites because of their emphasis on externals. They cleaned the outside of the cup but ignored the filth inside it (Matt. 23:25). They tithed the smallest of garden seeds but neglected the weightier requirements of the law like justice, mercy, and faithfulness (Matt. 23:23). Jesus' ultimate exposure of hypocrites was to portray them as "whitewashed tombs, which look beautiful on the outside but on the inside are full of dead men's bones and everything unclean" (Matt. 23:27, NIV).

---

meant more for Jesus than for the people. Jesus' critics were looking for such opportunities to denounce him.

Little wonder Jesus denounced the ruler and others of like mind as hypocrites who were more concerned with their animals than they were with people. A provision in the law allowed care for animals on the Sabbath day but provided for the healing of persons only in cases of dire emergency. They would have loosed their ox or donkey from its stall and taken it for a drink of water on the Sabbath but would have left this woman in physical and spiritual bondage. And she was a daughter of Abraham, one of their own. One can only imagine how severe the reaction had she been of another nationality.

When we consider how this incident applies to us today, we might at first dismiss it. After all, we do not have synagogues, and we do not worship on the Sabbath. Now we have churches, and Sunday, the first day of the week, is our day of worship. God decreed for his human creation a day of rest, a day for emphasis on the sacred instead of the secular. This one day out of seven was given to acknowledge our status as creatures of God and to emphasize our special relationship to God. Jesus established the church to continue his work in the world. The church is his people called out of the world to fulfill his purpose until he comes again. The Lord's Day

*Rules often handicap our ministry to people.*

is special. The church is an institution of sacred purpose. But the intent of God is perverted when the day and the church become ends rather than means. God's concern is for people. Both the church and the Lord's day are for God's glory and for the good of people.

Do we allow rules and traditions to hinder our ministry to people? Do we care more about the way we do something than we care for the people we are called to serve? If you doubt that, think about how difficult it often is to change something an established church does on Sunday. One Sunday, we decided we would not have a printed order of service for Sunday morning. The intent was to be more spontaneous in our worship. An outcry came from some who just could not be secure without a bulletin in hand to guide them. Churches have actually divided over the times for services, over the order of worship, and over singing choruses instead of the accepted hymns. Could one reason new churches often grow faster than older ones be because they do not have a backlog of tradition to maintain? They can be more sensitive to what ministers to people.

Order and tradition are not necessarily bad. In proper perspective they are good. But they are not primary, not the main thing. People are primary. The church that is sensitive to God's leadership will continuously subject its rules and methods to the people test. If a program is not meeting the needs of people, discard it. If rules are getting in the way of ministry, change the rules. Never think the way we have always done it is necessarily God's way or the best way. This does not mean you should rush out and change everything. Change for the sake of change is unwarranted. Changing to minister better to people is wise.

*God's concern is for people.*

Think about how you would react if someone like this woman interrupted a worship service in your church. Would you be embarrassed? Would you think, "Surely this could wait till the service is over"? Or would you think, "Here is an opportunity to do the work of God while it is day, to help a fellow human before the night comes and opportunity is gone?" (See John 9:3–5.)

## Ministry to People Glorifies God (13:17)

Glorifying God is our calling as God's people. Paul stated an abiding principle when he wrote, "Whatever you do, do it all for the glory of God" (1 Corinthians 10:31, NIV). This applies both to individuals and to churches. God is glorified when the beauty of God's presence is made manifest. God is glorified when God's name is exalted. God is glorified in people more than in rules. God is glorified in ministry more than in traditions. God is glorified in mercy more than in methods.

God was glorified in the incident we are presently considering. When the woman who was healed straightened up for the first time in eighteen years, she praised God (Luke 13:13). She gave glory to God. She left no doubt as to who was the source of her liberation.

When Jesus challenged the callous attitude of the synagogue ruler and those who agreed with him, they were humiliated. They hung their heads. Other people in the synagogue were delighted. They rejoiced. They realized that what Jesus had done was wonderful. The word "wonderful" (13:17, NIV) can also be translated glorious. God was glorified, not only for the healing of this woman but for all the glorious things he was doing through Jesus to meet people's needs: forgiving sinners, feeding the hungry, healing the sick, restoring the fallen.

*Changing to minister better to people is wise.*

Acts 3–4 tells how Peter and John reached out to a beggar who had been blind from birth. This desperate man was healed in Jesus' name and began praising and glorifying God. The authorities who opposed Jesus' followers resented the apostles' act of mercy, and they ordered them arrested. They questioned Peter and John and ordered them not to speak anymore in the name of Jesus. The authorities dared not harm the apostles, for the people were praising and glorifying God for what had happened.

The early church was a God-centered, people-centered movement. It was a movement freed from the bondage of sin and legalism. People responded. The church grew. God was glorified.

## Case Study

Suzanne, a Christian member of another denomination, attended the Downtown Baptist Church on a Sunday morning with her friends. Downtown Church was observing the Lord's Supper. The pastor made it clear only immersed believers were invited to partake. This had always been the practice at Downtown Church. Suzanne was upset she could not participate with her friends. Her friends were embarrassed.

How could this situation be handled so as to avoid the resulting ill feelings?

## Help People the Jesus Way!

Tom Henderson is pastor of Heights Baptist Church in Temple, Texas. With the cooperation of other ministers and churches of the Temple area, Tom led in starting a ministry to people who were experiencing hard times. Food and clothes and money for utilities and emergencies are distributed through the ministry that is called CTLC—Churches Touching Lives for Christ. Tom solicited and received a one-time substantial gift from the Baptist General Convention of Texas, along with monthly financial support from Bell Baptist Association. This ministry is helping people the Jesus way. Jesus ministered to physical needs as well as spiritual needs. The gospel of Jesus Christ is shared with every person served by CTLC. Many have been won to faith in Christ, and some are now active in the churches of Temple.

God will bless a church whose priorities are in order. Love God! Love people! Glorify God! Minister to people!

## QUESTIONS

1. How do our Sunday activities preserve God's purpose in the Sabbath?

2. How should we observe the Lord's Day today?

3. Is it necessary for some to work on the Lord's Day? Who? Why? Why not?

4. What does our church do that is subject to change? What is not?

5. What are some of our practices that Jesus might call hypocritical?

## Focal Text

Luke 24:13–35

## Background

Luke 24:1–53

## Main Focus

As we experience the resurrected Jesus, we will make him known to others.

## Question to Explore

How can we more readily experience and more willingly share the resurrection of Jesus?

## Study Aim

To find ways to be more willing to experience and share the good news of the resurrected Jesus

## Texas Priorities Emphasized

- Share the gospel of Jesus Christ with the people of Texas, the nation and the world
- Equip people for ministry in the church and in the world
- Strengthen existing churches and start new congregations

LESSON SEVEN

# Experiencing the Resurrected Jesus

## Quick Read

We are more apt to share the gospel of Jesus Christ with others when we have a growing experience of the presence of our risen Lord.

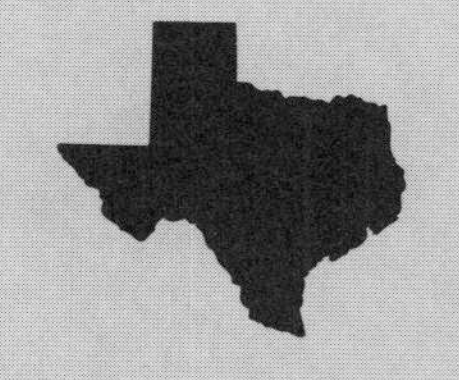

Rob Gunn is in the construction business in central Texas. Several years ago, he was attending a sales meeting in Dallas at the Anatole Hotel. Hundreds of people were there for Rob's meeting, along with hundreds of other regular guests at the hotel. One evening Rob got on the elevator to go to his room on the eighth floor. Another person was in the elevator. He was a tall, distinguished man who looked strangely familiar. Rob gave this man the once-over, trying to figure out who he was. When Rob arrived at his floor and the elevator doors opened, he turned to look one last time. The man realized Rob was struggling and came to his rescue. He pointed his finger at Rob and said, "Charlton Heston." Rob was flabbergasted as the doors closed behind him. He did not see the famous star anymore, but needless to say he had something to tell the other guests. The fact is, Rob is still telling that story today. Had the famous stranger not revealed his identity, Rob might still be wondering who he was.

This lesson is about two people who were once in the presence of a stranger they could not identify. After a while, the stranger revealed himself to them. That left them with a story to tell. In fact, people are still telling that story today.

## Disciples Doubt the Resurrection of Jesus (24:13–24)

"Now that same day" was the first day of the week (24:13, NIV; see 24:1). It was resurrection Sunday. Two followers of Jesus were returning home from Jerusalem. Emmaus was a journey of about seven miles. The exact location of Emmaus is uncertain, although Dr. William Barclay in his "Daily Study Bible" on the Gospel of Luke confidently locates it west of Jerusalem. If that is right, they would be travelling toward the setting sun. They had not yet realized that behind them in Jerusalem, the sun had risen on a new day. Jesus had been raised from the dead.

As the two walked, they talked about what had transpired in Jerusalem. The language indicates it was an animated conversation, perhaps sprinkled with debate as to their understanding of what had happened and what, if anything, it meant. Suddenly, Jesus, yes Jesus himself, whom they believed to be dead, overtook them and listened in on their discussion. "They were kept from recognizing him" (24:16, NIV), indicating they were not ready to receive the full truth of the resurrection. Seeing Jesus was the last thing they were expecting.

Jesus asked, "What are you discussing together as you walk along?" (24:17, NIV). One of the two is identified by name, Cleopas. We know nothing of him apart from this event. The other disciple remains anonymous. It has been generally accepted that the person was another man, but the possibility that this was Cleopas' wife has also been suggested. The two disciples seem to have been impatient with the interruption. They paused to respond. Their faces betrayed the sadness they were feeling. If this intruder had been to Jerusalem, surely he would know the things that had happened there in the preceding days.

*The resurrection is central to our Christian confession of faith, but affirmation does not always mean assurance. When the first disciples of Jesus heard the report of his resurrection, they doubted and only later believed.*

Jesus wanted to hear from them how they understood what had happened. He proceeded to draw them out by asking, "What things?" (24:19, NIV). Their commentary on what had happened concerning Jesus of Nazareth was a statement of faith but also a confession of doubt. With others, they believed Jesus was a great prophet. He had taught with such convincing authority. His mighty works could not be denied. They had hoped "he was the one who was going to redeem Israel" (24:21, NIV). To *redeem* means to ransom or liberate at a cost. Cleopas and his companion most likely understood redemption as the deliverance of the nation from Roman oppression. What could they now conclude but that their hopes had been forever dashed by the crucifixion of their leader? That their priests and rulers had handed him over to die added to their crushing disappointment.

*It is one thing to say the Lord is risen; it is more convincing when we can say from our own experience that he is risen indeed!*

What had happened earlier on that third day since his death further confused them. Women who were among the followers of Jesus had gone to the tomb where Jesus was buried. The body was gone. The tomb was empty. But that was not all; the women had reported seeing angels who told them Jesus was alive.

Other disciples then visited the tomb. We know, not from Luke but from John's account, these others would have been Peter and another disciple, likely meaning John (John 20:3). They likewise found the tomb empty. The body of Jesus was not there.

## Resurrection Appearances

How many times, in what order, and to whom did Jesus appear after His resurrection? Harmonizing the Gospels at this point is difficult. The differences in the reports are what you would expect from independent witnesses and makes it certain there was no collusion on their part.

There were five appearances on resurrection day. The first was to Mary Magdalene (John 20:1–18), the second to other women who came to visit the tomb (Matthew 28:1–10), the third was apparently to Peter (Luke 24:34), and the fourth to Cleopas and his companion (Luke 24:13–32). Fifth, Jesus appeared that evening to his disciples in Jerusalem (Luke 24:36–43; John 20:19–25).

A week later he appeared to the disciples again in Jerusalem (John 20:26–31; 1 Corinthians 15:5). Later he appeared to seven disciples at the Sea of Galilee (John 21) and again to the eleven on a mountain in Galilee (Matthew 28:16–20). Forty days after the resurrection, he appeared to the disciples in Jerusalem, and they followed him to Bethany (Luke 24:50–53; Acts 1:3–8). There he ascended into heaven.

In 1 Corinthians 15:5–8, Paul indicated Jesus appeared to more than 500 followers and also to James (Jesus' brother), without giving time or place for either. Lastly, he appeared to Paul at his Damascus road conversion, which would have been after the ascension.

---

The women's report was discounted. Jesus had talked to his disciples about being raised from the dead, but they could not believe it had really happened. Apparently at this point Cleopas and the other disciple from Emmaus said their sad good-byes to their fellow disciples and began the sad journey home, their fondest dreams destroyed.

Some would conclude that people of the first century were more gullible than we are today with our scientific understanding. The fact is, they were no more receptive to the supernatural than are we. Jesus' followers had no inclination to believe in his resurrection. Those who knew him best were skeptical. Their worldview did not include the concept of resurrection. It is the same today. How remote is the possibility that some have suggested, that these dejected disciples stole Jesus' body and then made up the story of his resurrection. That was the last thing on their minds.

That the secular world today would deny the resurrection of Jesus is not surprising. Neither should it be shocking that those who love and serve Jesus wrestle intellectually and spiritually with this marvelous truth. The resurrection is central to our Christian confession of faith, but affirmation does not always mean assurance. When the first disciples of Jesus heard the report of his resurrection, they doubted and only later believed.

Former President Jimmy Carter, a devout Christian who is a Baptist, has shared his intellectual struggle to believe in the resurrection. He has reported that as a youth he would end every prayer before saying, "Amen" with "And, God, help me believe in the resurrection."[1]

When I have struggled with faith, it has been helpful for me to pray as did the man who asked Jesus to heal his demon possessed son: "I do believe; help me overcome my unbelief" (Mark 9:24, NIV)!

## Disciples Experience the Risen Lord (24:25–32)

Jesus addressed the two Emmaus disciples' report of how they had responded to what had happened in Jerusalem. He was concerned with their reluctance to believe. Not only had Jesus shared with his followers in advance about the necessity of his suffering, this theme often had been addressed in the Old Testament. Had they been more diligent in their study of Scripture, they could have been spared their present discouragement. One of the most convincing evidences that Jesus is the Messiah is how he fulfilled Old Testament prophecy.

Prophecies pointing to Jesus can be found throughout the Old Testament. None are more direct than the portrayal of the suffering servant of Isaiah 53. This passage makes clear not only that he suffered but also that he suffered for us and our salvation. When read to the end, that great chapter makes it clear that the servant's suffering would not be the last word. It clearly points to God's ultimate victory through the Christ.

*The living Lord comes to us as he did to those on the road. He comes to us in our sorrow and pain. He comes when we are discouraged and distressed. He comes to calm our fears and bring us peace.*

As the three of them continued their walk to Emmaus, Jesus walked the two through Scripture. He started with Moses, the first great prophet and the human author of the first five books of the Bible, and continued through the remainder of the Old Testament, showing how it pointed to him. This must have been the greatest Bible study of all time. We are prone to wish we could have listened in on that session with the great teacher. We would like to have the list of passages he used that clearly pointed to his birth, ministry, death, and resurrection. The fact is, we do have that study. We have the New Testament that from Matthew through the Revelation affirms Jesus to be the Christ who fulfills the Old Testament messianic hope.

When they left Jerusalem with a seven-mile walk ahead of them, the two disciples must have dreaded the journey. They were physically tired and emotionally drained. But as this one, still unknown to them, began to explain the Scriptures, they forgot their exhaustion and arrived all too soon at the place where they were staying. No wonder they insisted Jesus not continue to journey this late in the day. "Stay with us," they pleaded (Luke 24:29, NIV).

Jesus stayed, and the three shared a meal together. The two must have considered it strange when the invited guest took the role of host, but they did not object. It seemed so natural for him to give thanks for the bread, break it, and share it with them. Then it happened. Their eyes were opened. They recognized him; it was Jesus. Hearing the first report of the resurrection had not convinced them, but now they had experienced his presence. Jesus made himself known to them in the sharing of a simple meal.

*We have a message to proclaim, to share, to shout from the housetops.*

The affirmation of the resurrection of Jesus comes to us through the testimony of witnesses, through the power of the written Word of God, through individual and corporate worship, and through observing the Lord's Supper, to cite a few ways. The living Lord comes to us as he did to those on the road. He comes to us in our sorrow and pain. He comes when we are discouraged and distressed. He comes to calm our fears and bring us peace. When he comes, we know that he is alive. We know him through the revelation of his person.

The arguments for Jesus' resurrection should be given due consideration. The evidences are many and persuasive. It makes sense to believe God raised Jesus from the dead. Furthermore, to believe that makes sense of everything else. But intellectual assent to the fact of resurrection is not primary. Belief is a matter of the heart that involves the mind and more. When our faith falters, the way of the Emmaus disciples is open to us. We can converse with Jesus through prayer, and we can hear from him as he speaks to us from the Word. And when Jesus comes, our hearts will burn within us, and we can shout for joy. He really is alive!

One more thought before we turn from experiencing the resurrection to sharing it. Remember, the theme of the unit of study of which this

## Case Study

Arthur is from a Christian home. As a youth he accepted the belief of his parents and the teaching of his church about Jesus' resurrection from the dead. When Arthur left home after high school graduation, he was confronted with a worldview that denied the supernatural and scoffed at believing in the resurrection. How can we help Arthur deal with his skepticism?

---

lesson is one part is "Loving Every Person." The resurrected Christ comes alive for us when we serve him through serving others. When we reach out and minister to the "least of these" we will find him there. The total package is found in loving God and loving others.

### Disciples Share the Good News (24:33–35)

By the time the two disciples realized they were in the presence of the risen Lord, he was gone from their sight. Jesus had accomplished his mission in appearing to them. They were now fully convinced he was alive. Have you ever been tired, then something exciting happened, and you experienced a burst of energy you did not realize possible? That is what happened to these two. Only one thing for them to do; they must return to Jerusalem and share this experience with their friends. As I read it, they probably did not finish the meal they had started. Food could wait.

They had trudged along from Jerusalem to Emmaus. On the return trip, night already having fallen, they hurried. They probably had traveled that seven miles many times but never as fast as that night. They arrived breathless and found the other disciples of Jesus. When they burst into the room they found the others already celebrating and sharing the confirmed good news: "It is true! The Lord has risen and has appeared to Simon" (24:34, NIV). I like the King James wording here, which says, "The Lord is risen indeed." It is one thing to say the Lord is risen; it is more convincing when we can say from our own experience that he is risen indeed!

We wish we knew more about that appearance to Simon. All we know is that it happened earlier that day and is confirmed by Paul in 1 Corinthians 15:5. We do know that even as they were meeting together on that memorable day, Jesus appeared again. They responded with a mixture of fear, wonder, and joy. Jesus blessed and reassured them. He showed them his wounds and spoke to them again about how all that had happened was fulfilling God's plan.

Reliving the experience of that long past day is good for us. Read about it and think about it until you sense you are there with those first disciples in Jesus' presence. That is what we do when we celebrate his resurrection. Every Sunday is Easter Sunday for the Christian. The reason we meet on the first day of the week is because that is the day Jesus was raised. Too, when we meet in churches large and small and sing his praises and hear his Word, we identify with those disciples like Cleopas and the others. We have a message to proclaim, to share, to shout from the housetops.

## Go...Tell!

The message of the resurrection must not be kept in the church. It is for the world, all nations, every person. The Book of Acts is the second volume of Luke's contribution to the literature of the church. It tells the story of how these disciples spread the Word in Jerusalem, Judea, Samaria, and beyond.

The heart of their message was the resurrection of Jesus Christ from the dead. That is our message for a lost and waiting world. "If Christ has not been raised, your faith is futile; you are still in your sins. Then those also who have fallen asleep in Christ are lost. . . . But Christ has indeed been raised from the dead, the firstfruits of those who have fallen asleep" (1 Cor. 15:17–18, 20, NIV).

*The message of the resurrection must not be kept in the church. It is for the world, all nations, every person.*

This is what we are about as Texas Baptists. We must take the message out of the church into the streets. We must knock on doors, visit institutions, make use of the media, until everyone has heard that Jesus is alive. We must travel country roads, penetrate urban centers, and alert those in the suburbs. The Lord is risen indeed!

## QUESTIONS

1. Why did the two disciples not recognize Jesus?

2. How can we cultivate our experience with the risen Lord?

3. What for you is the strongest reason for believing in the resurrection of Jesus?

4. Why do you think Jesus made a special appearance to Simon (Peter)?

5. What are some ways we can share the good news of our risen Lord?

## NOTES

1. Jimmy Carter, *Living Faith* (New York: Times Books, 1996), 17.

## Focal Text

Luke 5:29–32; 14:12–15

## Background

Luke 5:27–32; 14:1–24

## Main Focus

As did Jesus, we should invite people whom others might call unacceptable to fellowship with the Lord and with us.

## Question to Explore

How does our guest list for fellowship with the Lord and with us compare with the guest list of people whom Jesus would invite?

## Study Aim

To compare our guest list with the guest list of people whom Jesus would invite

## Texas Priorities Emphasized

- Share the gospel of Jesus Christ with the people of Texas, the nation and the world
- Minister to human needs in the name of Jesus Christ
- Equip people for ministry in the church and in the world
- Strengthen existing churches and start new congregations

# LESSON EIGHT

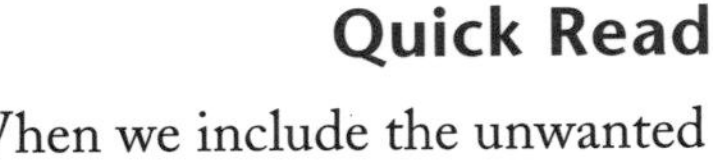


## Quick Read

When we include the unwanted in our circle of fellowship, we can know this is what Jesus would do, and we can be sure of his blessing.

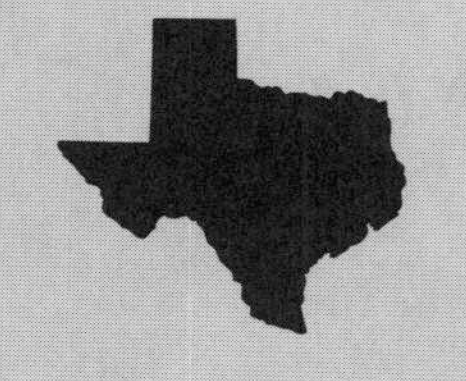

Harold Ellis is the founder and director of the jail ministry in Bell County, Texas. That ministry goes by the name J.A.I.L., for "Jesus Acting in Inmates' Lives." A recent innovation spawned by this creative ministry is a church for released offenders, their families, and other interested persons. The church is called the "Faith, Hope and Love Fellowship." This mission congregation of the First Baptist Church of Belton, Texas, has its own pastor and its own building. They meet on Tuesday nights, making it possible for the workers and members to be involved in other churches on Sunday. Harold calls this fellowship a stepping-stone church. The idea is to minister to the special needs of this group in a non-threatening setting until they are ready to be assimilated into more traditional congregations.

## Jesus' Invitation to Followship and Fellowship Is Addressed to All (5:29–32)

The two passages we focus on today—Luke 5:29–32; 14:12–15—revolve around social gatherings for meals. The first is a banquet given in honor of Jesus by his new disciple Levi (Matthew). The second is a dinner Jesus attended by invitation from a Pharisee. The emphasis in both cases falls on who was invited, who participated, and who was welcome. Both occasions turned out to be opportunities for emphasis on inclusion, especially of the outsider and the unwanted.

Obviously, the two incidents point beyond the immediate context. They contain lessons about the nature of the kingdom of God and lessons for the church of Jesus Christ. Shared meals, still today, represent some of the best opportunities for reaching out to and including others in Christian fellowship. To invite a person to an evangelistic service is one thing; it is quite another thing to invite a person to share in table fellowship. Table fellowship provides a more intimate setting where relating may occur at a deeper level.

Why is the disciple of Jesus better known as Matthew here called Levi? In the first century, people would often have an Aramaic or Hebrew name and a Greek name. That is the case with Matthew, known also as Levi. He appears in the gospel record here for the first time. He was a tax collector. Jesus passed by his office one day and invited Matthew, "Follow me" (5:27, NIV). Matthew responded immediately and became a disciple of Jesus.

Jesus' call of Matthew clearly indicates that Jesus was open to those who were not approved of or wanted by others. He reached out to those on the social fringe.

The twelve were an unusual mixture of people. Four were fishermen (Peter, Andrew, James, and John), and one was a Zealot (a radical nationalist). They were not well known. Their credentials were minimal. Matthew is well known to us because he wrote one of the four gospels. But initially, it was most likely a shock to everyone involved that Jesus called him.

The Jews hated the tax collectors. They considered tax collectors to be traitors. They had sold out to the Romans and were extorting their own people.

We should remember that the system of collecting taxes was entirely different from that of today. A dishonest tax collector could become very wealthy. He would pay his superiors an agreed amount and then pay himself commissions amounting to as much as he could collect over what he paid to those over him. The impression is that Matthew had wealth since he owned a house and could afford to give Jesus a great banquet.

*"The increasingly diversified population of Texas is projected to go over 20 million by the year 2000. This consists of about 11.3 million Anglos, 5.9 million Hispanics, 2.4 million African Americans, 500,000 Asians, and 60,000 American Indians."*
—U.S. Census Bureau projection for the year 2000

To that banquet, Matthew invited his friends, which for the most part would be other tax collectors. Apparently he wanted his old friends to meet his new friend, Jesus. This is evangelism at its best. New followers of Jesus will know more people they can introduce to Jesus than at any other time in their lives. And what better way is there to share a new relationship than in one's home where there is a sharing of food and friendship? This kind of informal setting is less threatening to the outsider and presents an opportunity to show unselfish concern for others.

The ever-present Pharisees and teachers of the law were watching Jesus' every move. When he befriended Matthew, they gasped. Now that Jesus was actually enjoying food and fellowship in Matthew's house, they erupted, complaining to Jesus' disciples, "Why do you eat and drink with tax collectors and 'sinners'?" (5:30, NIV). The mention of "sinners" indicates there were other undesirables at the banquet besides the tax collectors. These sinners were what we might refer to today as the "unchurched." They lived outside the influence of the rules and traditions, which to the

## Tax Collectors

The tax collectors of the New Testament, also called publicans, worked for the Roman government and were seen as traitors to their own people. The Romans delegated the collection of taxes to the highest bidders. Those who won the contracts hired others who did the actual work.

Zacchaeus (Luke 19:1–10) was "a chief tax collector and was wealthy" (19:2, NIV). Matthew was apparently of a lesser rank but still a man of substance. The collector exacted enough from the people to meet the demands of his contract plus whatever he could pocket for himself. Several senior officials would benefit from the commissions before the taxes reached their final destination.

The tax collectors were hated by the people and placed in the same category as sinners and harlots. While they were most despised for fleecing the people, they were also denounced for handling the blasphemous coinage of Rome with its pagan and idolatrous inscriptions. Furthermore, these infamous collectors were subject to bribes by the rich, thus increasing the financial burden of the poor and powerless. Is there any wonder Jesus was criticized for fellowshipping with the likes of Matthew and Zacchaeus?

---

mind of Pharisees governed one's relation to God. They did not adhere to accepted practice as understood by the teachers of the law.

Jesus responded to the criticism. "It is not the healthy who need a doctor, but the sick. I have not come to call the righteous, but sinners to repentance" (5:31–32, NIV). The proud, self-righteous, religious establishment thought their relationship to God secure. They had no sense of need. The tax collectors and sinners, on the other hand, were still open to God. They had no sense of being good enough. They could still acknowledge and confess need. Jesus delighted to spend quality time with and enjoy the company of this crowd.

### Jesus' Invitation to Fellowship Includes a Call to Repentance (5:32)

Any discussion of inclusiveness in the invitation of Jesus would be incomplete apart from affirming the importance of repentance. The gospel call is a call to repent. Our text is clear. Jesus said he had come to call "sinners to repentance" (5:32, NIV). John the Baptist, in announcing the dawn of the messianic age, declared, "Repent, for the kingdom of heaven is near" (Matthew 3:2, NIV). According to Mark, Jesus launched his ministry in

Galilee with the words, "The time has come . . . . The kingdom of God is near. Repent and believe the good news!" (Mark 1: 15, NIV).

Inclusiveness can degenerate into compromising the gospel demand for a changed life. Repentance is a word too often absent from modern calls to follow Jesus. A gospel that does not include repentance is no gospel at all, however. Seeker-sensitive churches, those who plan their services for the unreached masses, have been lauded and berated. Critics have at times been unfair, for many such churches are completely true to the gospel. Jesus was seeker-friendly. At the same time, he did not compromise with sinful behavior. In following his example, it is appropriate for us to use creative means for reaching the lost. To imply, however, that it does not cost to follow Jesus is not appropriate.

*Shared meals, still today, represent some of the best opportunities for reaching out to and including others in Christian fellowship.*

Earlier in Luke 5, Jesus called Simon Peter to discipleship (5:1–11). The Lord had been teaching from Simon's boat. When he finished speaking, he challenged Peter to put out into the deep water and let down his nets for fish. Peter resisted, for he had already fished through the night with no results. Still, he obeyed. When his nets filled with fish, he recognized he was in the presence of deity. Peter's reaction was, "Go away from me, Lord; I am a sinful man!" (5:8, NIV). Peter was humbled at this revelation of Jesus' person and power. Such is the appropriate response for all who are confronted with the gospel of God's grace. Jesus encouraged Simon and the others, "Don't be afraid; from now on you will catch men" (5:10, NIV). Peter and the others "left everything and followed him" (5:11, NIV).

Matthew's response to the call of Jesus was the same as Peter's. He "got up, left everything and followed him" (5:28, NIV). The forsaking of vocation in the cases of Peter and Matthew involved more than repentance, but not less. Does this mean all who would follow Jesus must leave their vocations? No! But it does mean all must renounce a life of sin and selfishness.

What then is the difference in following Jesus and conforming to the way of the Pharisees and teachers of the law? Is what we have in Jesus a new form of legalism? Not at all. Jesus called for faithfulness to the law of God and more. "For I tell you that unless your righteousness surpasses that of the Pharisees and the teachers of the law, you will certainly not enter the kingdom of heaven" (Matthew 5:20, NIV). The difference is understood when we compare repentance and reformation.

The Pharisees called for reformation, for conforming to the law as they understood and interpreted it. Jesus called for repentance, which means not only to turn from sin to God, but to change from the inside out. The Greek word behind the word "repent" means a change in one's mindset. Repentance is revolutionary change, which cannot be accomplished by firmer resolve but only by the power of God's grace and the indwelling, empowering Holy Spirit.

Evangelism can be defined as presenting the gospel in the power of the Holy Spirit and leaving the results to God. What this means to me is that if we are faithful to proclaim a complete gospel, one that includes repentance, we can know God's blessing and power will be at work in the hearts of those who hear. We can trust that people properly confronted with the claims of Jesus must either refuse his offer of salvation or receive it for the life-changing force it is. We know the difference it made in Matthew's life. We do not know the response of those tax collectors and sinners who attended Matthew's dinner. We understand, however, that this is an appropriate model for us as individuals and churches. We can open the doors to all who will come and know that God will, through our efforts, continue to call sinners to repentance.

## Jesus Blesses Those Who Include the Unwanted in Their Fellowship (14:12–15)

We turn now to Luke 14. Verses 1–24 describe a scene where Jesus was dining on a Sabbath day in the house of a prominent Pharisee. This was a set-up for entrapping Jesus. He was being carefully watched. A man with dropsy was there, which led Jesus to challenge the contention of the Pharisees that healing violated the Sabbath prohibition against work (see 14:1–6). When the Pharisees would not respond to his question whether it was lawful to heal on the Sabbath, Jesus healed the man. He then reminded them that if they had a child or an animal that fell in a well on the Sabbath they would rescue that child or animal. The Pharisees ignored him.

The guests continued to gather, and the time for the meal arrived. Jesus observed the behavior and the identity of the guests (see 14:7–11). He then set forth two important lessons, one for the guests and one for the host. The guests had scrambled for the seats of honor. Those special places would be at the head table if there was such or at any rate nearest the host.

Everyone wanted to be recognized as important. Jesus warned that if a guest took the place of honor on his own, the host might deem another guest to be more distinguished and ask the presumptuous guest to move. Since by that time all the other places would have been taken, only the lowest place would be left. The self-important guest would be humiliated. Rather, Jesus advised, take the lowest seat to start with. Then if the host sees fit, he will ask you to move up to a preferred place.

Thus, Jesus calls for humility. The self-centered person who presumes his importance will rightly be humbled, but the humble person will be properly exalted. Jesus was pointing to the way it is in the kingdom of heaven where God is the host. True humility is a signal virtue for those who are subjects of God's kingdom. Moreover, humility in a host would prevent him from making the mistake Jesus addressed next.

With the exception of Jesus, and perhaps the man with dropsy, this host had invited his friends and relatives, his kind. Jesus had a better idea for such an occasion. He challenged the host to move out of his comfort zone and "invite the poor, the crippled, the lame, the blind" (14:13, NIV). The guests at this meal were people of substance who could repay their host with a future invitation and would be expected to do so. Jesus called for including those who could not reciprocate. Then, Jesus indicated, they would be recompensed in the resurrection of the righteous, a reference to rewards bestowed by God at the end of the present age.

Jesus' mention of the resurrection of the righteous caused one at the table to comment, "Blessed is the man who will eat at the feast in the kingdom of God" (14:15, NIV). It was customary in Jesus' day to refer to the dawning of the messianic age as a banquet. This is what the speaker would have in mind. Jesus proceeded with a parable, which made it clear that many of those who had been invited to God's banquet would not be present. They would make excuses and miss the opportunity. Jesus'

---

## Application Actions

1. Reach out now to a person in your church who needs a friend.
2. Reach out now to an unchurched handicapped person who needs a friend.
3. Get involved in your church's ministry to visitors and new members.
4. Befriend the people who move into your neighborhood. Help them get acquainted with your community.

---

remarks can only be understood as referring to this present company of Pharisees and teachers of the law. Descendants of Abraham, they had been invited along with the patriarchs and prophets of old, but now that Messiah had come they had rejected him. These religious elite would be excluded from the Master's banquet, but others would be invited and would respond. The poor, the crippled, the lame, and the blind would be included. Servants would go out into the streets and roads and bring others in to share in the Kingdom of God.

## So What Does Jesus Think of Us?

The challenge for the church is to be inclusive. Too often, churches have been self-serving in their outreach. The temptation is to go first for those of like kind who can contribute to the growth and stability of the body. We give up too easily on those who are not comfortable with us and may seem out of place.

This lesson makes it clear that Jesus disapproves of a church that ignores any person or any group of people. Churches have been slow to reach out to minorities, the handicapped, the poor, and other identifiable groups. We have been slow to accept the unwanted when they do come, reluctant to embrace them as one of us and part of the family of God. We must not be satisfied with our attitude towards people until we see every person as a potential member of the family of God; until we can look each one in the eye and say sincerely: "God loves you and so do I."

## QUESTIONS

1. What did it mean for Matthew to leave everything and follow Jesus? What does it mean for us?

2. What are some strategies we can use to introduce our friends to Jesus?

3. Have you had lunch with any outcasts lately?

4. What persons or groups need our help but can in no way repay us?

# LESSON NINE

# What Are You So Happy About?

## Focal Text

Luke 15:11–32

## Background

Luke 15:1–32

## Main Focus

God is happy when people who are lost are found, and we should be, too.

## Question to Explore

What would it take for us to be as happy as God is about people who turn to God in faith? What response is appropriate to the grace of God?

## Study Aim

To acknowledge and accept the grace of God available to you and to all others

## Texas Priorities Emphasized

- Share the gospel of Jesus Christ with the people of Texas, the nation and the world
- Equip people for ministry in the church and in the world
- Develop Christian families
- Strengthen existing churches and start new congregations

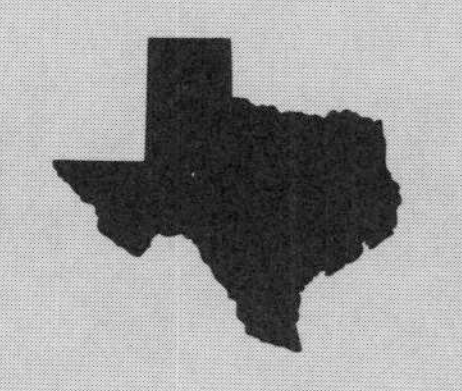

## Quick Read

God loves people who are away from him. He rejoices in forgiving those who return to him. He invites us to celebrate with him when the lost are found.

One Sunday morning the choir at our local Baptist church was singing an anthem and reinforcing its message with a simple touch of drama. One of the older and most respected men of the church dressed in the garb of a first-century father. A younger man from the congregation portrayed a wayward son. The father stood on the platform, placed his hands over his eyes, and peered longingly over the congregation and down the aisles of the auditorium. Right on cue as the choir sang, "Rejoice, rejoice, my son is coming home again," the son entered from the rear and started haltingly down an aisle. His clothes were tattered, his hair unkempt, his face and arms smudged and dirty. The father caught sight of the son and started running to meet him. He embraced him, put a beautiful robe on him, slipped a ring on his finger, and provided sandals for his feet. A holy hush fell over the congregation. People were moved. Tears of joy were shed. My only question: "How do we respond in the presence of the real thing?"

## God's Love Gives People the Freedom to Rebel (15:11–12)

This story of a prodigal son is surely the greatest and best loved of all Jesus' parables. One reason for its popularity is its remarkable portrayal of the love of God for all people. Perhaps it should not be called the parable of the prodigal son but the parable of the loving father or the parable of the forgiving father. The father is unquestionably the main character in this unforgettable story.

Jesus told three parables in Luke 15, the first about a lost sheep (15:3–7), the second about a lost coin (15:8–10), and the third, this one about a straying son (15:11–32). These parables answered a recurring criticism of Jesus by the Pharisees and teachers of the law that he befriended sinners and even ate with them (15:1–2). Jesus defended his association with sinners as a reflection of God's love for those who are away from him.

This parable is also impressive in the way it depicts us in our relationship to God. Jesus' parables are often like mirrors in which we can see ourselves. With a little imagination, we can see ourselves in the two sons: first in the rebellious prodigal; but alas, too often, in the resentful older brother. The younger son is representative of those who are away from God, separated from God's loving care. The older son is representative of the Pharisees and teachers of the law, Jesus' critics, who refused to rejoice in God's saving love for lost sinners.

Old Testament law decreed that the older son should receive two thirds of his father's estate (Deuteronomy 21:17). Hence, in a family of two sons, the younger would receive one third. Ordinarily an estate would not be divided until the father's death, but there were exceptions. The younger son's demand for his share is an indication of his displeasure with the father. He rejected his father's authority. He wanted to take control of his own life. He decided that he no longer needed the father who had loved him and provided for him through his early years.

Without debate, the father divided his property between the two sons. This action can only be understood as the way God deals with his human creation. We are created in God's image and at least a part of the meaning of that thought is that we are responsible. To be responsible we must be free. God did not create puppets or robots to manipulate. God created people who have the awesome power of choice to submit to God or to reject him. From our first parents we have inherited an inclination to sin and, indeed, "all have sinned, and fall short of the glory of God" (Romans 3:23, NIV). The story of this rebellious son has its roots in the Garden of Eden and is repeated in every succeeding person's life. The prodigal's story is our story. God loves us so much that God grants us permission to rebel against him.

*With a little imagination, we can see ourselves in the two sons: first in the rebellious prodigal; but alas, too often, in the resentful older brother.*

## God's Love Yearns for the Return of the Lost (15:13–20)

Inheritance in hand, the younger son took off for another country. He wanted to distance himself from his father and everything that reminded him of home. He would do his own thing, run his own life, and spend his time and money as he pleased. He "squandered his wealth in wild living" (15:13). The word "prodigal" means lavish, extravagant, and unrestrained. He wasted what had been given to him by a loving father. Wild living is irresponsible living. This rebellious son started out like the rich farmer in another of Jesus' parables (Luke 12:13–21), thinking he had everything he needed to "take life easy; eat, drink and be merry" (Luke 12:19, NIV). Like that same farmer, the prodigal son ended up playing the fool, not realizing that his life was not his own to do with as he pleased.

The prodigal's rebellion against his father led to ruin. All of the son's life, he had been in an environment where his needs were taken care of; now his world was a hostile place. His money was gone, the economy had turned sour, and there was famine in the land. His support system crumbled, and his friends deserted him. Where could he turn? He was so desperate he hired himself out to an employer who raised pigs. How low could he sink? Only as a last resort would a self-respecting Jew take a job feeding pigs. Swine were unclean animals, and working with them would be entirely unacceptable.

Whatever wage the prodigal might have received from working with the pigs was not enough. He was so hungry that what the pigs were eating looked good to him. The "pods" would be the seeds of the carob tree and not suitable for human consumption (15:16). His psychological state was such that it seemed to him the pig's life was better than his was. He was at the end of his rope. He was lost.

"He came to his senses" (15:17, NIV). He saw himself for what he had become and knew that he was not made for this. The younger son realized there was more to life than this degraded existence. He thought of father and home, where the lowest level of slaves had more than enough to eat.

The decision he made at that point was not easy. It is never easy to admit you were wrong. "I will set out and go back to my father" (15:18). He would ask to be hired as a servant; he would be a slave at the house

## Lost

Have you heard the one about the evangelist who knocked on a farmer's door and asked, "Are you lost?" The farmer replied, "Nope, I've lived here all my life."

This exchange is an example of how we sometimes fail to communicate with people we are trying to reach. What does it mean when we refer to non-Christians as the "lost"? Luke 15, along with 19:1–10, provides us with the clearest understanding we have of "lost" used in a doctrinal sense. The fact is, references to the "lost" are somewhat scarce in the rest of the New Testament. "Lost" is not a prominent category in the writings of the Apostle Paul. A form of the Greek word translated "lost" is used in 2 Corinthians 4:3, but the NIV translation there is "perishing." Other forms of the Greek word can mean to destroy, to ruin, to perish, and even to kill.

"Lost" is a dreadful word when, as in Luke 15, it clearly signifies separation from God and being on the way to ruin. "Lost" is a useful concept in sharing the gospel as long as people understand we mean "lost to God." The "lost" are those who need to hear the saving gospel of our Lord Jesus Christ.

where he had once been a son. He would throw himself on the mercy of his father. Would his father help him? The son could not know the answer to that question; he only knew the need that haunted him.

Not for one moment had the father forgotten his straying son. He had watched and waited and longed for his son to come home. While the son was still way up the road the father saw him, knew him, and ran to embrace him. What we have in this part of the parable is an unforgettable picture of a rebellious sinner's repentance met with God our Heavenly Father's forgiving love.

## God's Love Receives Sinners (15:21–24)

Dare we suggest that the father was the true prodigal in this story? Not if *prodigal* means waste and excess as concerning the son. Since, however, *prodigal* also means lavish and extravagant, it surely applies to the father's love. With every gesture and action the father took, he was declaring his love for a son who had rejected him and had squandered his inheritance. The father did not wait for the son but went to him. He did not walk; he ran. The son began to confess his sin and unworthiness and ask for the menial work of a lowly slave. The father interrupted with orders to the servants to bestow upon the returning prodigal the unmistakable marks of sonship.

*God did not create puppets or robots to manipulate. He created people who have the awesome power of choice to submit to God or to reject him.*

The father's embrace and kiss gave assurance that reconciliation was complete. The "best robe" was a garment of distinction and honor. The "ring" would bear the family seal and signify the authority that would belong only to a beloved son. Slaves would go barefoot, but not a son. The son must have sandals for his feet. The "fattened calf" was one that had been reserved for the most special of occasions. What a celebration for a son who had shown himself to be an ungrateful wretch! The son asked for mercy but received grace. Mercy is being spared the punishment we deserve. Grace is receiving far beyond anything we could ever deserve.

The message of the parable is this: Listen up, you Pharisees and teachers of the law who sneer at Jesus' association with sinners. God loves sinners and delights in their repentance and restoration to himself. To repent and turn to God as the prodigal did is to receive forgiveness and life.

## Case Study

Two church members led a young couple to Christ on an evangelistic visit. The couple came forward at the next worship service and were presented as candidates for baptism and church membership. They were regular in attendance for a while but then began to miss church services and eventually dropped out. When they were contacted as absentees, they indicated they had no friends at the church and did not feel comfortable and accepted there. What can we do to prevent this from occurring?

Can you see yourself in the prodigal son? Some would say without hesitation, "Yes, that is my story. I lived a wasteful and immoral life before becoming a Christian." Others may be thinking: "This is not my story. I do not identify with prodigal excess such as is depicted in this parable." Your story may be more like that of a rich young ruler who approached Jesus asking what he must do to receive eternal life (Luke 18:18–23).

The young ruler lived a moral life, but something was missing. What more could he possibly do? When Jesus invited him to forsake his obsession with wealth and let God be God, the young man turned away and continued to worship his wealth.

The fact is, we are all sinners by nature and by choice. Away with the tendency to categorize some as more sinful than others. All have sinned. All are separated from God. Your "distant country" is wherever you are until you are forgiven and received into the family of God. There is absolutely nothing you can do to earn God's favor. Only the grace of God can suffice for our salvation.

### God's Love Is Reason for God's People to Celebrate (15:25–32)

Happiness is in the air in Luke 15. Celebration is the mood from beginning to end. Three parties are given, one when the lost sheep is rescued (15:6), another when the lost coin is found (15:9), and a third when the lost son is restored (15:23). The atmosphere of rejoicing is by no means limited to those who people these parables. The greater joy is that celebrated in heaven in the presence of the angels of God (15:7,10). The reason for this transcendent delight is the repentance of just one sinner, the recovery of one person who was lost. Think about it! God throws a party in heaven to celebrate the rescue of one lost person!

But wait, the happiness is not universal. Who would not join in such a celebration? The older brother was not at the house when his younger brother returned. He was at work in the fields. As he approached the house after a long day's work, he heard the sounds of music and dancing; he asked a servant what this might be. When he learned they were celebrating his younger brother's homecoming, he got angry and refused to join the party.

> *The prodigal's story is our story. God loves us so much that God grants us permission to rebel against him.*

The father left the party to plead with him to join the festivities. The older brother refused. He had rather pout. He accused his father of neglecting him and favoring his younger son. He accused the younger brother of cavorting with prostitutes, something he could not have known. Remember that he received two-thirds of his father's property, and he had enjoyed the benefits of home all these years. But he saw himself not as a beloved son, which he was to the father, but as one who had worked for everything he had and therefore deserved everything he had received. He was a self-centered legalist. To him, his brother had not lived by the rules and therefore did not deserve the father's love.

Often, we end our treatments of the parable of the prodigal son with verse 24. That approach serves an important purpose but misses the point Jesus was making to his critics, the moralistic Pharisees and teachers of the law. The older brother represents their attitude toward sinners. They had a sense of religious superiority that, for them, justified their snobbish rejection of that unacceptable crowd.

Now, we must be careful lest we sneer at these ancient Pharisees and miss seeing our own image in the mirror Jesus is holding up to us. Are there elements present in our attitude toward others that make it difficult for us to celebrate the salvation of sinners?

## What Makes Us Happy?

If you have ever lost something of value like a wallet or a purse and then found it, you know how troubling a loss can be and how relieving the recovery. Recently, my eight-year-old granddaughter's new puppy was missing from her backyard home. The child's heart was broken; she was devastated. Her parents were distraught. She shared her loss with others.

In fact, she e-mailed us over thirty miles away to be on the lookout for her missing pet. We understood and shared her sorrow. After a while, the good news came. The lost puppy was safe with near neighbors. Everyone was relieved and happy. We did not get together for a party, but we certainly felt like celebrating.

Texas Baptists' number one priority is to share the gospel of Jesus Christ. Do we care that people are lost? Are we burdened for those who do not know Christ? Texas is a mission field, and the challenge of reaching our state for Christ is greater than ever. The times we live in call for a renewed sense of urgency both in reaching individuals for Christ and starting new churches.

Do we need to learn to celebrate with those who are saved? Do we need a heart change so we can share the Heavenly Father's joy over sinners who repent? I was in a church service recently where people made decisions for Christ. As they came forward to confess their faith in Jesus, others hurried from out of the congregation to welcome them, to stand with them, to embrace them, and to support them. It did not seem perfunctory or contrived. My heart was warmed.

God, forgive us when bad attitudes keep us from rejoicing with people God loves and forgives. God, forgive us when we take for granted any prodigal's return to his gracious embrace.

## QUESTIONS

1. Does the parable of the prodigal son tell your story? How? How is your story different?

2. What might have happened if the returning prodigal had met the older brother before he met the father?

3. How do you account for the attitude of the Pharisees and the teachers of the law?

4. What can I do to show my happiness for people who come to Christ?

5. Do you see yourself reflected in the attitudes of the older brother?

# Free Churches in a Free Society

Authorities arrested Reverend Joseph Bays for conducting worship services. During transport for trial, the six-foot, 200-pound Baptist preacher overpowered the guards. He escaped and eluded capture.

The town was San Felipe in Stephen F. Austin's Texas colony. Mexican authorities had charged Bays with violating Article 3 of the 1824 Constitution, "The religion of the Mexican Nation is, and will be perpetually the Roman Catholic Apostolic. The nation will protect it by wise and just laws, and prohibit the exercise of any other whatsoever." The tradition of church and state combined continued when Mexico obtained its independence from Spain in 1821. Although generous economically to Texas colonists, Mexico proved intolerant on religious liberty.

By 1830, about 20,000 immigrants had settled Texas, many from the United States. Based upon colonization laws, these settlers were to be Roman Catholics. Most were not, and there weren't enough priests to convert them. To obtain land, Frederick Ernst had to kiss the Bible and promise to become a Catholic when a priest arrived. But Frederick never converted. Another embarrassing issue concerned marriages. Only priests could perform ceremonies. Bypassing the process, many Texans signed marriage bonds. Z.N. Morrell wrote that after Texas' independence, he often officiated weddings with the couple's children as witnesses.

T.J. Pilgrim founded a Sunday School in San Felipe, with 40 members traveling up to 10 miles each way. The Empressario discontinued the services. Aunt Massie Millard organized the first prayer meetings in thickets while hiding during raids.

Officials often looked the other way as long as the Texans didn't commit theft or murder. However, times changed dramatically when Santa Anna made himself dictator of all Mexico. The colonists fought his harsh rule.

In the blacksmith shop of Baptist preacher N.T. Byars, Texans declared independence from Mexico on March 2, 1836. The bloody fight for Texas independence ended at the San Jacinto River on April 21, 1836. Texans had won both civil and religious freedom. Baptists constituted their first church in N.T. Byars' shop in old Washington. Citizens remained so committed to the separation of church and state that ministers could not serve in the legislature of the Republic.

Thank God for religious freedom.

—KATHY HILLMAN

UNIT 3

# Getting Your Priorities Straight

Priorities are choices. Christians must take a hard look at themselves, being bold enough to ask the tough questions to gain honest insight into personal desires, goals, and lifestyle. Inertia, doing nothing, is devastating and destructive. Desires must be evaluated against the instructions and examples of Scripture. Self-discovery, inspired by God's Word and His Spirit, should prompt a positive response. Godly priorities are forceful, positive, effective, strengthening, and helpful. Setting proper priorities helps solve personal and social problems and gives witness to our faith in Christ.

Our world is changing rapidly. The continued secularization of society, accentuated by rapid change, is dramatically affecting families, values, lifestyles, institutions, education, customs, leisure time, relationships, and every other part of our lives. The church, the body of Christ, is losing its influence. The trend is toward further moral erosion. People are empty and desperate for spiritual truths. The Christian community is not adequately offering answers.

So what are we to do? To adequately confront the world, we must look upward to our Lord, inward to our priorities, and then outward to others. Priorities motivate us and guide us to focus our energy.

Paul says in Colossians 4:5, "Be wise in the way you act toward outsiders; make the most of every opportunity" (NIV). It is not acceptable to see life as little more than taking advantage of our daily opportunities to increase our own personal enjoyment. We must place the priority on fulfilling our personal mission in Christ.

These four lessons focus on getting our priorities straight in four areas in which people are especially challenged today. Priorities Christians need to emphasize include:

- putting possessions in their place (Luke 16:13,19–31)
- living life with gratitude instead of believing life—or God—owes us (Luke 17:11–19)
- being humble in spite of how hard that is given how wonderful (we think) we are (Luke 18:9–14)
- being faithful to Jesus, who faithfully gave himself to God in the fullest commitment possible (Luke 22:39–48,54–62)

## Focal Text

Luke 16:13,19–31

## Background

Luke 16:13–31

## Main Focus

Loving things is a poor substitute for loving God and people.

## Question to Explore

What is an appropriate place, if any, in a person's life for the desire for wealth?

## Study Aim

To identify the extent to which my priority is on loving wealth rather than loving God and people

## Texas Priorities Emphasized

- Sharing the gospel with everyone in Texas, the nation and the world
- Ministering to human needs in the name of Jesus Christ
- Equipping people for ministry in the church and in the world

# LESSON TEN

# Put Things in Their Place

## Quick Read

Money is a major concern of almost everyone. The parable of the rich man and Lazarus helps us define the proper focus and use of our financial resources. God's grace is extended to all regardless of their status.

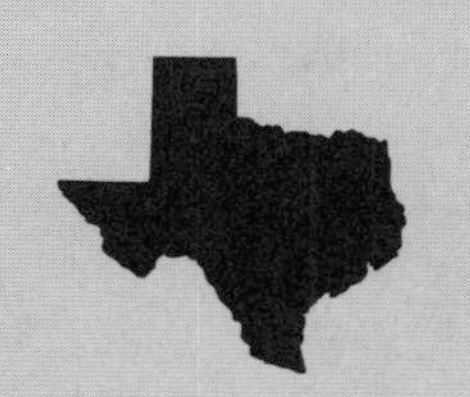

A few years ago, I led a mission group to St. Petersburg, Russia. While there, we made a brief visit to a portion of the Hermitage, the great museum in St. Petersburg. Never have I seen such a display of wealth, consisting of magnificent art, gold, gems, sculptures, and frescoes. It was awe-inspiring. The museum was a depository for the wealth of the Romanov family, who ruled Russia for 300 years. For me, however, the riches of the Hermitage stood in sharp contrast to the poverty of Russia's people.

The rich man Jesus told about in Luke 16:19–31 is not the only person with the desire for ceaseless gratification of the desire for material things. A wealthy Baptist layman was dying. A friend of mine went to see this layman on his deathbed. The man had grown consistently weaker and now could only gasp an audible whisper. To hear him, my friend bent over with his face next to his. The last thing he heard the wealthy man say before he died was this: "I want some more money." One cannot help wondering whether as he died he was expressing the major desire of his life.

We Texas Baptists have a great challenge ahead of us, that of claiming Texas for Christ and ministering to human needs. This challenge cannot be met without the faithful generosity of all Texas Baptists. Reaching the lost often means meeting human needs first. Putting money in its proper place affords its use for the glory of God. Our giving patterns reflect our attitude toward God and others while our spending patterns reflect our true values.

## No Divided Loyalties (16:13)

Luke 16 begins with Jesus' parable about a landowner who employed a dishonest servant or steward. Facing dismissal, the dishonest servant called all of the landowner's debtors and bargained with them. He agreed to reduce their debt to the landowner in order to win friendship so he could secure his future after his dismissal. The landowner commended the dishonest servant for his shrewdness in providing for himself and others. One should not make a case here for being admitted to heaven because of one's generosity (see 16:9). Using one's wealth, however, to build relationships for future benefits is wise. The trustworthy servant is one who uses material blessings wisely to relieve human need and to benefit others.

Jesus brought the parable to a climax by clearly stating that we cannot serve both God and money—the vision of God and the vision of greed—

at the same time. We can serve God, though, by using wisely the money with which God blesses us. If we use wealth only for our own personal satisfaction, we are not serving God, but money.

Luke 16:1 indicates that Jesus was teaching his disciples as he told the parable and made these statements. Luke 16:14–15 points out that the Pharisees also were listening—and "were sneering at Jesus" (16:14, NIV). Thus, Jesus was directing these teachings, including the parable of the rich man and Lazarus in 16:19–31, to the Pharisees. They are described in verse 14 as people "who loved money" (16:14, NIV).

*Throughout history, the poor have suffered because of the greediness and selfishness of the wealthy.*

Our world is caught up in the desire for affluence. The most common priority of the American dream is wealth, money, possessions. Affluence commands the time, talent, energy, and focus of many people. The encouragement of greed by human nature and capitalism affects us and our society. Indeed, greed drives the forces of our economy to make our affluence the envy of the world. We are a nation of consumers. Rather than consuming to live, we live to consume. Consumerism shapes our attitudes, guides our lifestyle, and molds our personalities. It defines our use of time, the number of children we have, the financial goals we set, and the relative status we achieve. At the same time, it contributes to the failure of families and distorts our value system. This emphasis on consumerism is not merely the background against which we live our lives; it is so much in the foreground that it dominates our lives. It is America today.

American churches often patronize the process of consumerism and legitimize participation in it. The church finds it easy to accommodate a blend of culture and biblical truths. The affluent culture tempts the Christian church with sweet promises of success similar to the way sex is used in selling soap.

In many cases, we identify far more closely with the rich man than with Lazarus. The poor are uncomfortable in our churches, and our budgets show little evidence of a concern for benevolent deeds. The church is often wealthy with its programs but weak in its charity. The scope of ministry to human need sometimes is narrowed in the name of focus marketing. The economically disadvantaged are left out of life and often left out of the church. Grace and mercy are denied to the less fortunate.

The parable we are about to study challenges our affluence and our consumerism at the point of our Christian faith. Intrinsically, there is nothing wrong with money itself, but we struggle with its purpose. The purpose of money to serve our Lord is lost when money is used mostly to satisfy our own urges.

## The Devaluation of Money (16:19–21)

This parable is connected to the previous parable in 16:1–8 as a poignant illustration of how people and society degenerate when money is placed above human beings in priority. Luke 16:19–21 also illustrates the erroneous philosophy that wealth is a sign of God's blessings.

Money, misused, will often bring corruption and terrible social consequences. Perhaps using a local experience which the Pharisees and disciples would recognize, Jesus painted a picture of a man who was so absorbed in his priorities and luxuries that he excluded God and his responsibilities to other people. As they listened, the Pharisees would not have been able to escape Jesus' condemnation of them for their wrong use of money and their missed opportunities for relieving human suffering.

*The last thing he heard the wealthy man say before he died was this: "I want some more money."*

The rich man has traditionally been called Dives, from a Latin word meaning "rich," as used in the Latin Vulgate translation of the Bible. Dives lived sumptuously every day of his life. He was totally disconnected from people in need. He lived in his big house, lounged in elegant clothing, and ate the most delicious food available.

Outside the rich man's gates was a beggar named Lazarus. He was poorly clothed, sick with sores, and miserable from his hunger. Dogs were his only friends, and they made him more miserable by licking his infected sores.

# Hell

The Greek word for "hell" in Luke 16:23 is *hades*. Both the King James Version and the New International Version translate *hades* in this verse as "hell," and it obviously is a place of punishment. With dramatic impact, Christ brought to the attention of the Pharisees that the place where the rich man now found himself was a horrible place for anyone, including themselves. This passage shows that upon death both Lazarus and the rich man immediately received their eternal reward, heaven or hell, and that the condition could not be reversed.

As Dives went in and out, he saw the beggar at his gates but otherwise completely ignored him. Dives was so self-absorbed that Jesus suggested that even one resurrected from the dead could not redirect his priorities (16:31). Tragically, Dives' self-interest denied him his own humanity. His fellow human beings in need were no more to him than dogs that roamed the streets and scavenged for their existence. There was no apparent feeling of sympathy or compassion for Lazarus as an individual. Even though the rich man had ample resources to do something about Lazarus' needs, he did nothing.

*Reaching the lost often means meeting human needs first.*

Dives may have been more disconnected and without conscience than he was cruel. Living in an affluent neighborhood often means never putting a face or a name to poverty, squalor, filth, pain, and hopelessness. Rather than have the poor man removed, perhaps the rich man was content to let him eat scraps with the dogs. Throwing out leftovers may have been Dives' contribution to Lazarus' poverty. If even that occurred, more than likely it was the work of the kitchen help, not Dives directly, however. Apparently, Dives had no personal involvement or direct contact with this unfortunate man. Dives is like those in every age who are rich and live in luxury but do little or nothing to relieve human need.

*If we use wealth only for our own personal satisfaction, we are not serving God, but money.*

In America, poverty and human need continue to be appalling. Many people, including children, continue to live in poverty. A recent report indicates that the financial boom of the 1980s and 90s reached only the top 5% of the households in America. Between 1983 and 1995, the rich saw an increase in net worth of 17.4% adjusted for inflation while the bottom 40% of American households saw a collapse of approximately 80% in net worth. One percent of the rich in America hoards 40% of the wealth, double the percentage of 1976. [1] America, with all of its wealth, is part of a worldwide problem of hunger, disease, poor health care, and malnutrition.

These figures show that the Dives-Lazarus contrast was not just an issue in ancient Israel. What can we do? At the very least, every church in Texas ought to have an offering for the poor and hungry to be used on the local, state, and national level. Other ways of ministering include clothes closets, food pantries, Christian Women's Job Corps, and many other ways. Unfortunately, the church, too, has difficulty looking past its stained-glass windows at the needs of people. A comprehensive approach is needed that includes churches, individuals, government, private institutions, and businesses.

Where does generosity begin? Generosity, as a priority, begins in your head, with your thoughts. How can you determine whether money is more important to you than people? Consider questions like these: How do you think about or react to human need and suffering? Is there compassion in your heart for those in need? You know your priority is not people when you do not feel their hurt, when you turn away from the needy when you see them, when you are prejudiced against their poverty, and when you are without courage to minister to those in need. You can change the way you think and act about your resources by putting God and others first.

## The Evaluation of Consequences (16:22–26)

The parable of the rich man and Lazarus is disturbing because of the emotion one feels in seeing the contrast of the rich man and the poor man. It is also disturbing because of the description of the suffering the rich man endured in hell.

*You can change the way you think and act about your resources by putting God and others first.*

Lazarus died and angels took him to heaven—expressed as "Abraham's side" (16:22, NIV). His death came early from unattended disease and unsatisfied hunger. Lazarus' body probably was not buried but taken to the city dump and burned. If so, such a picture makes the drama of the rich man's torment in hell even more compelling. It's another illustration of the bad things that occurred to Lazarus in his life in contrast to the good things that happened to the rich man. The situation was reversed at their deaths (see 16:25–26). At best, Lazarus' body would have been placed in a potter's grave without fanfare. Lazarus was considered completely worthless.

On the other hand, Dives died and would have had a splendid burial. His family, friends, neighbors, and colleagues would have attended to the rich man. There would have been flowers, memorials, crowds of mourners, and a grand processional to the place of burial. He and his wealth would be missed.

Note in verses 23–24 that Dives was "in hell," "in torment," and "in agony" (NIV). Death for him was a rude awakening, a wake-up call of the greatest magnitude. He discovered things about life and death that he never had imagined. He found that he had been a fool. "Torment" describes the intensity of his new knowledge and experience. Dives found that death for him was not the end but a threshold of entry into everlasting suffering. He was able to see across the great chasm and observe the comforted Lazarus. The rich man was envious of the poor beggar who had reaped the rewards of heaven.

*A deacon in our church said to me recently, "I do not want to stand before the Lord in the day of judgment and have him call me 'stingy.'"*

The rich man's priorities changed in at least these ways. First, instead of money, Dives wanted the same comfort, joy, and pleasure that Lazarus had in heaven (16:23). Second, instead of luxury, Dives wanted relief from the "agony in this fire" (16:24, NIV). Third, instead of extravagance, he wanted to get the message to his brothers (16:28).

In spite of the prayer of Dives, nothing could change his eternal condition. This is the consequence of godless, selfish living in this world.

Dives had had such wonderful opportunities to bless others, but he had failed to do so. His life was wasted on his wealth. The result of his way of life stands as a warning. The graces of the rich are an inadequate substitute for the wonderful grace of God. The rich man had confused material wealth with spiritual blessings and was blinded to the real message of

---

## How Serious a Problem Is Materialism?

1. To what extent do you think materialism is a serious problem?

   Not serious  Somewhat serious  Serious  Extremely serious

2. *USA Today* reported that some of the world's wealthiest people say they would give $640,000 for a place in heaven.[2] What do you think of that?
3. How does your emphasis on spiritual growth compare to your emphasis on material things? When compared to your emphasis on material things, your emphasis on spiritual growth is

   Much less  Less  About the same  Much greater

---

salvation by grace through faith in God. In this life, Dives had everything money could buy, but in death he had nothing but torment and memories of what might have been. Judgment was certain, with dreadful finality.

## The Valuation of Others (16:27–31)

Now the rich man's priorities changed dramatically. Verses 27–31 show us that Dives for the first time had concern for others. This change in priority expressed itself toward those he loved the most. With the eyes of his heart opened, Dives begged to spare his brothers on earth the torment he would endure forever. He gave ardent testimony of his new experience and spiritual discovery. He sought to warn his kin of the impending consequences of social injustice and unfaithfulness to God.

Think about it. In light of what happened to the rich man, isn't it extraordinary that we who believe do so little to live and share our faith?

*We can easily determine whether we love money more than we love God and our fellow human beings by the way we use our financial resources to help those in need.*

God is sending the world to Texas. Many faces of different races and languages are included in the rapidly expanding population growth. We urgently need an experience with Christ that will lead us to become bold witnesses for our faith. We also urgently need biblically based stewardship. A deacon in our church said to me recently, "I do not want to stand before the Lord in the day of judgment and have him call me 'stingy.'" Our giving reflects the value we place on the efforts of our church and denomination to reach our world for Christ.

In verse 29, "Moses and the Prophets" (NIV) refers to the Old Testament. Father Abraham's message in verse 29 to the rich man was that the rich man's brothers had sufficient witness in God's written word about the way God wanted them to live their lives. They needed no other messenger.

Dives responded, "No, Father Abraham . . . but if someone from the dead goes to them, they will repent" (16:30, NIV). The fact is that they did have someone who had been raised from the dead. Jesus raised Lazarus of Bethany (John 11). The response of the Pharisees and Jews was a plot to kill Jesus (John 11:45–53) and to kill Lazarus (John 12:9–11). Miracles do not necessarily bring belief. One can still ignore the signs and the conviction of the Spirit of God. It is easy to think that another startling sign or miracle might be convincing.

People are not saved, however, by waiting for more information and more acts of God's grace but by responding to the information and grace they already have received. The Samaritan woman waited for Messiah, saying, "When he comes, he will explain everything to us" (John 4:25, NIV). She did not recognize that she was speaking directly to the Messiah at that very moment. God comes to us in our lives in many ways and opens up opportunities for faith. Let us seize the day and make Christ our Savior and Lord. To wait is dangerous for both the rich and the poor.

In this parable, Christ challenges our thinking about money. How can we evaluate the place money has in our lives? One way of determining whether we love money more than we love God and our fellow human beings is to assess the way we use our financial resources to help those in need. Money is not the problem. People are the problem and the solution.

## QUESTIONS

1. Is it accurate to conclude that if you do not respect the needs of others, you do not respect yourself?

2. What are some uses of your financial resources that you believe would please God?

3. Why do you think giving money is sometimes so difficult for us to do?

4. What motivates a rich person like the person in this parable to live such a selfish life when so many people are in need?

5. Why is it that some are so overwhelmed with the needs of others that they feel hopeless and do nothing?

6. How prevalent is the feeling that the needs of others are someone else's problem—city, county, governmental agencies, etc.?

7. What excuse did the rich man offer when he faced God?

8. To what extent do you think that Christian individuals and the church identify with Dives rather than Lazarus?

9. Do you know individuals whose lives are at risk because of poverty?

## NOTES

1. "10,000 Dow hides flaws in market boom," *Dallas Morning News*, April 6, 1999.
2. *USA Today* "Snapshot," http://www.usatoday.com/snapshot/news/nsnap03.htm, accessed May 1999.

## Focal Text

Luke 17:11–19

## Background

Luke 17:11–19

## Main Focus

Rather than seeing life as a debt owed to them, people of genuine faith are grateful for life as an undeserved gift of God.

## Question to Explore

What do you think life owes you?

## Study Aim

To express earnest gratitude for God's blessings in your life

## Texas Priorities Emphasized

- Share the gospel of Jesus Christ with the people of Texas, the nation and the world
- Minister to human needs in the name of Jesus Christ
- Develop Christian families
- Equip people for ministry in the church and in the world

# LESSON ELEVEN

# Recognize That Life Doesn't "Owe You One"

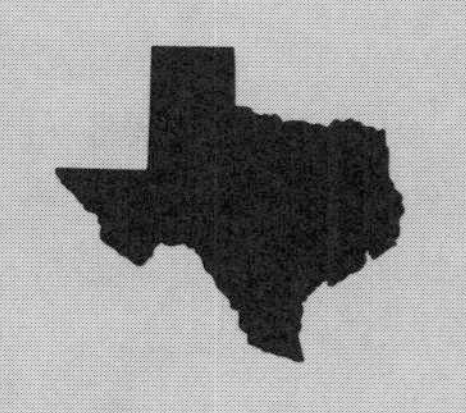

## Quick Read

Jesus places great value on gratitude and misses it when it is not expressed. Only one of the ten lepers came back to express gratitude for Christ's blessing and to give praise to Him in worship. Thanksgiving is to be a resource for life rather than a burden of inconvenience.

Tonu Lehtsaar, a graduate student at Baylor University, grew up near the Golgotha Baptist Church in Tartu, Estonia. His father was responsible for maintenance on the church. When the Communists took over in 1944, they charged his father for a crime of which he was not guilty and shipped him to Siberia to work in the mines. Four years later, they told him that they had made a mistake and that he would be released. He had no money, though, and had to work another two-and-one-half years to get enough money for his journey home. At home, he never talked about what happened while he was in Siberia.

One day Tonu and his father were walking to the church. Fresh snow had fallen. Tonu's father spoke to him about the unusual beauty of the day and how it reminded him of a day in Siberia as he and others walked to the mines. He mentioned how he remembered the sun reflecting off the snow in Siberia, making a beautiful scene for which he was so grateful. There was one difference, though. There in Siberia the snow was red, not white.

Tonu asked his father, "Why was the snow red?"

His father replied, "Because we did not have any shoes." Though he had walked in the snow without any shoes and with bleeding feet, he remembered with gratitude that it was a beautiful day.

Regardless of the circumstances of life, one can always find something for which gratitude can be expressed. Rather than asking, "Why did this happen to me?" Tonu's father looked around and said, "What is there to be grateful for?" By being grateful, he was not a victim but a victor. When gratitude is a valued priority, life can always have its moments of joy.

On the other hand, some people evidently think that life "owes them one." This attitude can generate from a sense of haughty arrogance, a complaint about one's condition in life, or both. We see this thought process in action when one says, "I deserve this."

Feeling that life "owes you one" is a seedbed for temptation and sin. Some of the greatest mistakes, misdeeds, and failures occur when one gives in to self-serving ideas or self-pity. Convincing oneself that money, sex, power, position, or possessions are deserved is a product of this state of mind.

This treacherous, dangerous experience of feeling that life owes one something can be very subtle. It may be that many of the moral failures of faithful Christian people, including ministers, come when they are exhausted and depressed from too many hours of effort and too little rest. In that condition, they say to themselves, "I deserve this." They then become involved in something that ultimately is destructive to them and to others. Guard against such thoughts, for the results can bring not only failure but ruin.

Rather than seeing life as a debt owed to them, people of genuine faith are grateful for life as an undeserved gift of God. Thanksgiving is a resource God gives us to avoid temptation, complaining, and character failure.

The story of the ten lepers is an actual event in the life of Jesus. The details of the story contain several surprises. Healing ten men at once, from a distance, is unusual. Too, in light of the repulsiveness of leprosy, with all of its hideous physical consequences, it's surprising, too, that there was only one thankful person of the ten who had been healed.

## A Condition That Prompted a Call (17:11–13)

Comparing Luke to the other three gospels indicates that Luke leaves out some events that evidently took place between Luke 17:10 and 17:11. During this time, Jesus raised Lazarus from the dead (John 11). Jesus then traveled to Ephraim and stayed there with his disciples. From there, he began again his final journey to Jerusalem and death. On the way, Jesus encountered the ten lepers. The experience occurred along the border between Samaria and Galilee (see Luke 17:11).

*Thanksgiving is to be a resource for life rather than a burden of inconvenience.*

Leprosy was an ancient disease that slowly destroyed and disfigured the body. The disease was so dreaded that the sight of a leper could cause revulsion and nausea along with pity and fear. Lepers lived as best they could away from people. Society treated them as outcasts. No physical condition in ancient times could equal the plight of those with leprosy. They were hopelessly locked into an incurable disease from which there was no known escape other than supernatural intervention.

These ten men had banded together because of their common malady. Respectfully, "they stood at a distance and called out . . . " as their hearts held on to hope (17:12, NIV). The distance reduced the lepers to misfits with medical and social needs. Luke's description suggests that they kept on begging loudly. Their howling cries provide insight into their own self-pity and despair. Their call to Jesus for mercy also indicates their recognition of Jesus' reputation and power (see 17:13).

## We Can Be Grateful

Texas Baptists have much for which we can be thankful. Included are such blessings as these:

- church membership is growing
- new churches are being built
- budget and mission support is escalating
- institutions are stronger
- resources for benevolent causes for all ages are expanding
- leadership in the Executive Board staff is outstanding
- mission opportunity through volunteers finds strong support
- inclusiveness is encouraged for all types of worship styles
- Great Commission evangelism and discipleship have been made our priorities
- opportunities for theological education for all academic levels are being provided
- strong and urgent work is being done in reaching the many ethnic populations
- lay theological mentoring studies are moving forward
- many avenues of ministry are being expanded
- church and pastoral support is being strengthened
- the use of technology is being intensified

Shouldn't we be grateful to God for God's blessings?

### A Compassion That Prompted a Command (17:14)

Jesus evidently was moved with compassion by seeing these diseased men. There is no indication that Jesus touched them as he touched the lepers in 5:12–15. He simply spoke the miracle into existence. He commanded them, "Go, show yourselves to the priests" (17:14, NIV). No calling for faith and no words about being cleansed are recorded. The fact that the lepers obeyed would imply great respect and faith in Jesus and his power, however.

In 5:12–16, Jesus first cleansed the leper and then sent the leper to the priest. Here, Jesus sent the ten lepers to the priest, and on the way they were healed. The difference between the miracles may suggest nothing of consequence. One can only guess that the difference in the two incidents lay in the men's hearts or in attendant unspecified circumstances.

Jesus told these men to go to the priest so that the priest could pronounce them clean. According to Mosaic Law (Leviticus 13:45–46; 14:1–9), the priest served as the local health official who would issue a health certificate verifying the cleansing. With faith, they obeyed. Somewhere along the road on the way to the priest, that thrilling, indescribable moment came when they realized the leprosy was gone. The Great Physician had healed their decaying bodies and freed them from the torment of a living hell. Jesus' command was all that was necessary to provide the physical healing. The command was given out of Jesus' heart of compassion and sympathy.

*Tonu asked his father, "Why was the snow red?" His father replied, "Because we did not have any shoes."*

## A Conscience That Prompted a Contact (17:15–18)

One of the lepers, and only one, came back to give thanks to Jesus. By coming back, this person acknowledged the source of his blessing.

Note that he took the time and made the effort to show his gratitude. What he did reminds us that it takes time and sacrifice to be grateful. Expressing gratitude is often inconvenient and time consuming, but the one leper who was healed came back to thank Jesus face to face. He "threw himself at Jesus' feet and thanked him . . ." (17:16, NIV). Gratitude and joy go together like a hand and a glove. This man was joyfully grateful.

Consider several observations about this experience and what it teaches us about gratitude. First, gratitude is most meaningful when it is demonstrated by actions. One of the ten came back to pour out his gratitude to Jesus. The physical action he took grew out of the real, flesh-and-blood, physical healing he had experienced. A message for us is that although it is good when gratitude is a thought, a conviction, or an attitude, it is better when it is more. Gratitude should be an act, not just a thought. Being grateful in mind is commendable but even more so is taking the time and trouble to express it personally. The miracle was the physical healing, but the victory was in the man's inward integrity that was appreciative enough to turn around and run back to Jesus. This one man had become something greater. He received the complete blessing, physically

*Thanksgiving is a vital part of our prayer life.*

and spiritually. He refused to take for granted the blessing he had received; he acted on his gratefulness, showing gratitude for the giver as well as the gift. The healed man may have had family to go and see, friends to look up, a neighborhood to visit, a home to return to, and children to raise, just like the other nine. First, though, he took action to express thanksgiving directly to Jesus, the Great Physician, who had blessed him. He was an honorable man of gratitude.

*Feeling that life "owes you one" is a seedbed for temptation and sin.*

Second, showing gratitude is important, even if doing so requires time and energy. Jesus had given the leper his health, exactly that for which he had prayed. He would have been aware of the effort and energy required for the healed leper to come back and give thanks. On the other hand, he also would have been aware of the greatness of the deliverance he had provided to the lepers. Such thoughts are behind Jesus' question, "Where are the other nine?" (17:17, NIV).

Thanksgiving is a vital part of our prayer life. Coming to the Father and giving thanks for his wonderful and powerful blessings will invigorate our praying. Jesus set the example for us. When he was raising Lazarus from the dead, he stood before the tomb and prayed. His prayer included these words, "Father, I thank you that you have heard me" (John 11:41, NIV). The Father is observant if and when we offer him prayers of thankfulness from a grateful heart. When we go day after day without giving thanks to the Father, we are no better than the nine ungrateful lepers whom we love to condemn.

*...the person whom we might least suspect to recognize the greatness of God's grace may be the one who does and is grateful for it. . . . The one who was grateful was a Samaritan.*

Third, the person whom we might least suspect to recognize the greatness of God's grace may be the one who does and is grateful for it. The passage notes that the one who was grateful was a Samaritan, who was an outsider or foreigner. For a Samaritan to be part of the group of ten lepers would have been thought strange, for Jews and Samaritans hated one another. Their racial and religious prejudice was heated and intense. Presumably the other nine were Jews, supposedly more aware of religious values. Luke evidently intended to make the point that proper and grateful response to the miracle was not from expected sources but from those whom the privileged Jews would despise. The condition of the heart was more important than race or religion.

This foreigner understood God better than those who worshipped there. This message would not be well received and is perhaps a prophecy of Israel's rejection of Christ in Jerusalem that would lead to his death.

*Rather than seeing life as a debt owed to them, people of genuine faith are grateful for life as an undeserved gift of God.*

As lepers, the Jews and the Samaritan were united in their common misery. Often, when individuals are reduced to their common humanity, they forget the issues that divide them and no longer quarrel over them. Perhaps the grateful attitude of this Samaritan was what prompted his acceptance into the group. Outwardly, he was the most unlikely of the ten. Inwardly, he spoke the spiritual language of the human heart.

A person whom I admire greatly is a young woman named Lizzie Phillips. I served as pastor to her parents when she was born. Her father, Gary Phillips, is the Financial Officer for *The Baptist Standard*. She was born blind and with other physical deformities. She is currently a student at Howard Payne University where she is excelling in her academic, artistic, and social life. She has a beautiful voice and an attractive personality. After more than two dozen surgeries on her eyes and legs, hundreds of visits to doctors, many medical procedures, and much medication, she still

## Grateful

| Ten Things for Which I'm Grateful | Whom I'm grateful to | Have I Thanked Them? |
|---|---|---|
| 1. | | |
| 2. | | |
| 3. | | |
| 4. | | |
| 5. | | |
| 6. | | |
| 7. | | |
| 8. | | |
| 9. | | |
| 10. | | |

lives in constant pain. Still, however, she is positive and thankful. Whenever she has the opportunity, she gives praise and glory to God for God's blessings and gifts.

To capture the spirit of Christ means being thankful in attitude regardless of the circumstances. To be thankful occasionally is not enough; gratitude is a lifestyle and reflects the prioritizing of this Christian value. Thankfulness is not a fair weather friend but is around in adversity as well.

*. . . Gratitude should be an act, not just a thought.*

Blessings in life are pleasurable and come from different sources, such as opportunities, unexpected income, answered prayers, achievements, recognition, and even tragedy. We should give thanks for all our blessings.

Christians understand the meaning of giving thanks far better than the secularist. The value of gratitude is appreciated most by those who have been redeemed. Gratitude is learned but also inspired by the Spirit of God who lives in us. One learns it, feels it, and knows it.

## A Conviction That Prompted a Conversion (17:19)

Jesus said, "Rise and go; your faith has made you well" (17:19, NIV). Herschel Hobbs has pointed out that the Greek word for "made you well" can mean *to heal of disease* or it can mean *to save.*[1] Since all of the ten were healed of leprosy, it would seem reasonable to conclude that the one who came back was not only healed but saved. He received far more than physical healing but spiritual healing as well. He was cured of leprosy and also saved unto eternal life.

*Gratitude is the heart of the Christian faith because it is the most appropriate conscious response to our salvation and the sacrifice of Christ on the cross.*

Gratitude is the heart of the Christian faith because it is the most appropriate conscious response to our salvation and the sacrifice of Christ on the cross. The Pharisee's approach reminds us that ingratitude can be cloaked in the language of gratitude. The Pharisee prayed, "God, I thank you that I am not like other men. . . ." (18:11, NIV).

An ungrateful heart contributes to the ills of society. No missile can protect society from the consequences of ingratitude, no church can survive with ungrateful people, no family can remain intact without thankful members, and no individual can please God with an ungrateful attitude. Christianity itself can not function or succeed without the presence and power of gratitude. So, are you grateful for God's blessings, or do you think life "owes you one"?

## QUESTIONS

1. How does an ungrateful heart contribute to the ills of our society?

2. How may an ungrateful heart contribute to personal depression?

3. Why would it be correct to say that gratitude is a barometer of the soul?

4. How can one know whether one is genuinely thankful?

5. Would the thankful heart be more grateful for the giver or the gift?

6. In what ways are worship and gratitude bound together?

7. In what ways can gratitude turn trouble into triumph?

## NOTES

1. Herschel Hobbs, *An Exposition of the Gospel of Luke* (Grand Rapids: Baker Books, 1966), 250.

## Focal Text

Luke 18:9–14

## Background

Luke 18:1–14

## Main Focus

Recognizing one's need of God's mercy and extending mercy toward others characterize genuine humility.

## Question to Explore

How can we strive to be our best before God and at the same time avoid believing we are more worthy of God's love than other people are?

## Study Aim

To recognize why everyone approaches God only on the basis of God's mercy and describe how this truth affects life

## Texas Priorities Emphasized

- Share the gospel of Jesus Christ with the people of Texas, the nation and the world
- Equip people for ministry in the church and in the world

# LESSON TWELVE

# Be Humble in Spite of How Wonderful You Are

## Quick Read

Humility in response to God's mercy is the key to our relationship with God, our prayer life, and our behavior. It is a value that commands a place of priority. Good work is never the basis of salvation. Only when we humbly throw ourselves on the mercy of God can we be saved and submit to his Lordship.

A young man had responded to God's call to preach. He was to preach his first sermon. He entered the pulpit with pride and arrogance and began to proclaim his message. When he had finished, he felt like a failure. He had disappointed himself and the congregation. Leaving the pulpit, he lowered his head in complete humility. His father, with a sense of wisdom and experience, told him, "Son, if you had gone up like you came down, you would have come down like you went up."

Humility is an approach to life that is very difficult to master. One problem in doing so is that once you have humility, you cannot be proud of it. If you are, you have lost it!

To understand the heart of God is to cherish the value of humility. Humility is an ultimate virtue and is the common ground between human beings and God. Only when you value it and have it are you willing and worthy to approach God.

## A Startling Contrast (18:9–10)

The parable involves two very different people, a Pharisee and a tax collector. Both were in the Temple to pray and worship. The faithful Jew prayed three times a day. To go to the Temple to pray was considered even more worshipful. Jesus likely directed the parable toward the Pharisees, who "were confident of their own righteousness and looked down on everybody else" (18:9, NIV).

Pharisees means "the separated ones." They were a religious group and political party in New Testament times, and they included some of the priests and scribes. The Pharisees insisted on the strict observance of God's laws. They had their roots in the Hasidim movement of the second century B.C. At that time, rather than giving in to the influence of the Hellenists who were trying to force Greek culture on the Jews, the members of the Hasidim insisted on living according to Jewish ritual and teachings. So, growing out of this movement, the Pharisees found respect and status and received much popular support as they insisted on strict observance of the laws and rituals of Judaism. The Pharisees gained a favored position over the other religious parties and won representation on the Sanhedrin, the ruling body of the Jews.

The Pharisees were heroes of the disciplined, godly life. They were champions in the struggle for morality and for maintaining Jewish customs. They were the most highly regarded of the sects of Judaism.

Some of the Pharisees, however, became haughty and self-righteous in their attitude toward all others, especially those who could not or would not keep the law as well as they did, like publicans and prostitutes. Further, although the Pharisees were good at keeping the law, their hearts were motivated by the people's praise rather than by zeal for God. Most of them were staunch enemies of Jesus and often received his rebuke and verbal chastisement (see Mark 12:38–40; Luke 11:37–52; 20:45–47).

*To understand the heart of God is to cherish the value of humility.*

In contrast to the Pharisee was the disreputable tax collector. The Roman government contracted the collection of its taxes to businesspeople. These businesspeople were responsible for paying a certain sum into Rome's treasury (called the *publicum*). These businesspeople were known as publicans, and they usually were Gentiles. These publicans then employed tax collectors to work the customhouses and enforce payments of the various taxes. Included were land taxes, poll taxes, Temple taxes, import taxes, road taxes, bridge taxes, and more. The citizen could pay thirty to forty percent in taxes.

The tax collectors themselves were usually from the community in which they lived and were well known. They extracted fraudulent taxes, brought false charges, overcharged, engaged in extortion, provided hush money, and in general operated Mafia-style as racketeers. Tax collectors gathered more than was required and put the overage in their own pockets. In addition, tax collectors were hated as traitors who had loyalties to Rome. They were cursed, despised, and avoided.

For Jesus to praise the prayer of a tax collector and condemn the prayer of a Pharisee would have been beyond belief. It would be difficult to suggest a greater contrast between the moral and the immoral, the accepted and the rejected, than this contrast between the Pharisee and the tax collector. Jesus in effect placed a no-good, cheating, Roman-sympathizing scoundrel on a higher spiritual scale than the Pharisee, a morally upright, upstanding citizen, a leader in the community and in his religion. Unbelievable!

## A Self-righteous Condition (18:11–12)

Jesus' parable lets us look into the heart of the Pharisee through the Pharisee's prayer. There were Pharisees, no doubt, who were humble, like Nicodemus (John 3:1–21), but not this one. This Pharisee was representative of most of them. He was totally and completely into himself. Four times in his brief prayer he used the personal pronoun "I" (Luke 18:11–12, NIV). The Pharisee acknowledged God but then talked about himself and to himself. In essence, the Pharisee's prayer indicates that he knew about God but worshipped himself. His relationship with God went no deeper than a legalistic knowledge and mental affirmation.

The Pharisee's prayer tells us that he looked down on others as sinners and condemned them. He certainly considered himself more worthy than they were. All of his prejudices of class and race were wrapped up in his assessment of other people in his prayer. He simply named what was to him the worst of the lot. He pretended no intention to involve himself in their needs. With his own needs met and position established, he tried to make himself look good by criticizing others. Standing in a prominent place in the Temple, he prayed an eloquent recital to himself in which he extolled his own righteousness as his offering of worship. He felt that God and the others in the Temple were very fortunate to have someone like him leading the prayer.

*. . . The Pharisee's prayer indicates that he knew about God but worshipped himself.*

On the surface, the Pharisee was the prime example of religious achievement and moral behavior. I believe that he really was not a robber, thief, evil doer, adulterer, and that he did tithe and fast. He was faithful to his religion, a patriot of his country, an example in his community. As viewed by himself and others, he was an outstanding citizen and religious leader.

So what was the problem? Mainly, he depended on his goodness for his merit and position. He failed to recognize and acknowledge his own deep

## Humility

The words "humbled" and "humbles" in Luke 18:14 (NIV) are from the same Greek word. The word means *to bow down, to make low, to humble.* The emphasis is on action as well as attitude. Christ was humble in both ways—action as well as attitude (Philippians 2:7–8; Matthew 11:29). Humility in one's relationship to others is referred to in Philippians 2:3, "Do nothing out of selfish ambition or vain conceit, but in humility consider others better than yourselves" (NIV).

Humility in one's relationship to God is submission to the grace and will of God, as Luke 18:9–14 exemplifies.

need of God. How could he be humble before God when he knew himself to be so wonderful? He couldn't and wouldn't. Furthermore, his motivation for keeping up appearances was to be recognized and applauded. It was all about *him*.

The Pharisee was careful to name the sins in which he did not participate. He arrogantly extolled his virtues. He did more than the law demanded, implying that God "owed him." In his prayer of pride, he thanked God that he was not like this tax collector, a sinner. The Pharisee named the tax collector as one of the types of individuals he despised.

Did the Pharisee, in his self-righteous pride, actually pray? Are there times when prayer is offered in church when the sins confessed are only the ones in which the one praying did not participate? God is not pleased when we refuse to deal with the sins in our life, whatever they are.

## A Sanctifying Contrition (18:13)

The prayer of the tax collector lets us look deeply into *his* heart, too. There was passion in his words that expressed feelings of grief and pain. The tax collector was involved in a base, bad profession that was fueled by greed, dishonesty, and inhumanity. He was a person of few if any virtues. He was a sinner, and he rightly deserved God's condemnation. No one knew such things any more than this tax collector. The tax collector, however, came to the Temple to pray for God's mercy while the Pharisee came to the Temple only to make an appearance. In humility, the tax collector approached God, appealing for God's mercy and not pointing out his own goodness. He did not feel comfortable being in the presence of God or the Pharisee. He "stood at a distance," because of his humility and feelings of unworthiness (18:13, NIV).

*Both the Pharisee and the tax collector got their prayers answered.*

Notice the differences between the tax collector's prayer and that of the Pharisee. First, the tax collector prayed not to himself but to God. Second, he compared himself with no one. Third, he confessed his own sinful nature instead of talking about somebody else's sins. He prayed as if he were the only sinner in the world and no one was as depraved as he was. A fourth difference is that he was humble. He would not even lift his head to look up. His physical demeanor told of the condition of his soul. He "beat his breast" in anguish and contrition (18:13, NIV). He prayed not to be heard by people but to be heard by God. He was so contrite that he could not help but pray honestly out of the depth of his spirit.

The Pharisee felt that God owed him something for his goodness while the tax collector believed that except for the mercy of God his soul would be lost in hell. The tax collector compared himself only to the righteousness of a Holy God. The tax collector's approach to God was just the reverse of that of the Pharisee.

The prayer of the tax collector was this, "God have mercy on me, a sinner" (18:13, NIV). The tax collector was burdened in his heart about his sinful past—cheating, dishonesty, and racketeering. His life was a wreck, and he had no peace of mind. With candor and honesty, he expressed the insight of every person who looks honestly into the face of our Lord. Sensing the purity of God's holiness in relationship to our sinfulness, all we can do is cry out for mercy.

To understand ourselves through understanding God is to recognize that sin is the most significant problem in life. Job said, "I am unworthy—how can I reply to you?" (Job 40:4, NIV). David cried, "Have mercy on me, O God, according to your unfailing love; according to your great compassion blot out my transgressions" (Psalms 51:1, NIV). Isaiah prayed, "Woe to me! I am ruined! For I am a man of unclean lips" (Isaiah 6:5, NIV). Peter fell at Jesus' knees and begged, "Go away from me, Lord; I am a sinful man" (Luke 5:8, NIV). This is what occurs when a sinful person meets God in humility.

The tax collector's humility and recognition of his sin is how we know he met God that day while the Pharisee did not. While the Pharisee used the name of God, he never saw himself as a sinner. The tax collector was so overwhelmed by his sin that he would not even look up toward God. He felt that nothing in his life was worthy of God's mercy.

*We all can and must come to Christ in the same way, praying the same prayer—* Be merciful to me, a sinner.

God is always merciful, without our having to ask God to be so. People need simply to recognize God's mercy, which is already available. The tax collector understood that he could seek the mercy of God in any situation. He sought God's forgiveness.

The word translated "have mercy on" (18:13, NIV) is the verb form of the Greek word for *mercy seat*. The mercy seat was part of the Ark of the Covenant in the Jewish Temple. On the Day of Atonement, the mercy seat was sprinkled with blood from an innocent, perfect animal as a substitute for the people's sins. It became the instrument of forgiveness for sin. God looked down between the wings of the gold angels on each side and saw the sacrifice of the victim rather than the sins of his people. With this background to the word the tax collector used, we can see that the prayer of this tax collector expressed a profound understanding of the way of forgiveness through the crucifixion and death of Christ.

## A Surprising Commendation (18:14)

The Pharisees and others who listened as Jesus told the parable did not expect what was about to take place. The drama in the parable had a surprising ending. Christ commended the humble tax collector and condemned the self-righteous Pharisee. Consider the consequences of their respective commendation and condemnation.

First, both the Pharisee and the tax collector got their prayers answered. The Pharisee got his recognition by people, which is what he really wanted, and the tax collector was justified before God, which is what the tax collector wanted. By looking down in humility, the tax collector looked up. By admitting his sinfulness, he received mercy. Through his humility, he was exalted.

*Our relationship to God does not depend on our strengths and achievements but on God's love and mercy.*

Second, your station in life makes no difference in God's willingness to extend mercy to you. When you reach out in humility for the mercy of God, you will receive it. We all can and must come to Christ in the same way, praying the same prayer—*Be merciful to me, a sinner.* This is the only way that forgiveness is possible and redemption can be received.

What about us—you and me? Humility is difficult to define and even more difficult to live. We may bring it out occasionally to impress someone, but then it is not humility, is it?

Humility is not a favorite virtue these days. Humility does not fit the world's concepts of prestige, authority, and power, in which self is valued over others. Humility is often seen as implying inadequacy and lack of self-worth.

Biblical humility, however, is the inward virtue that translates into complete dependence on God and submission to his Lordship. Such humility is freedom from arrogance. In a sense, this kind of humility may be the foundation of all other virtues. Our relationship to God does not depend on our strengths and achievements but on God's love and mercy.

Our model for humility is Christ. He was humble in his incarnation (see Philippians 2:1–11), in his servanthood (see John 13:1–17), and in his death (see Luke 22:42). He expects his followers to accept and live the virtue of humility, too. In fact, it is impossible to have holiness without humility. Humility glorifies Christ while conceit leads others astray. Christian humility exalts and places others first rather than self.

As I stood on the porch of the home of church members and waited for them to answer the doorbell, I noticed a pear tree laden with fruit, its branches nearly doubled over and broken. I noticed that the limbs that bent the most and hung the lowest were the ones with the most fruit. Christians who are humble, putting others first, are also the most fruitful. It works at home, in the church, and in the world.

## QUESTIONS

1. What are some indications of pride and self-centeredness in the lives of church people?

2. To what extent do you ignore sin in your life when you pray?

3. Why do you suspect that some people think they have a privileged relationship with God?

4. How can goodness keep one from salvation?

5. Why do people appeal to their goodness when asked about their relationship with God?

6. Are there church members who look down on others with this attitude: *I thank God I am not like that person of that racial background—or like that poor person—or that prisoner*?

7. Defining humility as total dependence on God and putting others first, how humble are you?

## Focal Text

Luke 22:39–48, 54–62

## Background

Luke 22:39–62

## Main Focus

Jesus, in contrast to Judas and Peter, exemplifies the faithfulness to God to which we should commit ourselves.

## Question to Explore

What motivations encourage our commitment to genuine discipleship? What motivations obstruct such a commitment?

## Study Aim

To determine to grow in my commitment to faithfulness to the Lord

## Texas Priorities Emphasized

- Share the gospel of Jesus Christ with the people of Texas, the nation and the world
- Equip people for ministry in the church and in the world
- Strengthen existing churches and start new congregations

LESSON THIRTEEN

# Stay Faithful to the One Who'll Never Let You Down

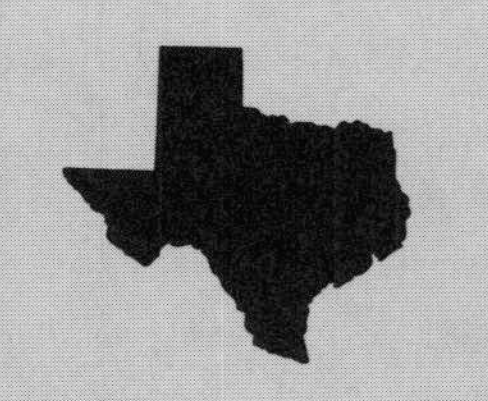

## Quick Read

Strength for faithfulness comes from those things that motivate and encourage us. Examining the experience of Jesus' preparing for his death and crucifixion and the betrayals by Judas and Peter can lead to some extraordinary discoveries about motivation and encouragement that can make a difference in your faithfulness.

Z. N. Morell came to the Texas frontier in 1835 to preach to the unsaved. Texas Baptist historian Leon McBeth calls him "the greatest pioneer preacher in Texas, and one of the greatest in America."[1] He was born in South Carolina and served as a pastor in Tennessee. He came to Texas with a vision on his heart and the faithfulness to achieve it. Facing the dangers, he fought off painful injuries, weakening diseases, human enemies, harsh environments, meager supplies, and more. He was rebuked and called a fool, but he obeyed the voice of God to preach Christ to Texas. He rode his mule to preach wherever anyone would listen. He laid the foundation for churches, associations, and Christian education while preaching Christ and affirming Baptist doctrine. Morell's faithfulness to the calling of God overcame all adversities as a frontier Baptist missionary. This is the kind of faithfulness that sets an example for all Texas Baptists.

## Priorities That Undergird Faithfulness

The pressure was on as Christ approached Calvary. Death was approaching, angry and belligerent crowds were growing, Jewish leadership was increasingly antagonistic, and emotional stress was mounting. Searching for strength, Jesus sought and used those things that would bolster and encourage him at this critical time. We can see at least four motivational forces in action in this remarkable experience.

*1. Place (22:39).* The first resource for Jesus was a special place called Gethsemane. Are there places in your life that add to your sense of communion with God? Jesus sought out his special place, Gethsemane, where he would find the resources of solitude, isolation, and beauty as he met the Father face to face.

Once while browsing a book in a tourist center in Edinburgh, Scotland, I found a reference to my family name. Researching further, I found the connection to a Scottish clan and read that the old castle was still standing and occupied. It took a day of hard driving and persistent inquiry to find the location. Looking for direction, I interviewed a neighbor near the castle. She informed us of the location of the family stone, the castle, and the hill at a nearby lake where the family gathered when under stress or attack. She explained that this hill became the crucial point for making decisions and planning strategy in difficult times.

Gethsemane was such a place for Jesus and his disciples. Here Jesus sought resources and strength to achieve his ultimate victory of redemption.

Gethsemane was a garden on the Mount of Olives. Luke simply calls it "the place" (22:40, NIV). Jesus and his disciples had been there many times ("as usual," 22:39, NIV). It was usual for Christ to find a quiet place and usual for him to use Gethsemane for solitude, prayer, and communion with the Father. Luke 21:37 tells us that Jesus was teaching in the Temple but that each night he would go to the Mount of Olives to sleep and rest. This would explain how Judas knew where to find him (John 18:1–2).

*Are there places in your life that add to your sense of communion with God?*

As a teenager, I found a place of prayer in the nearby forest. I would nestle down between the shoulders of a hollow in the side of a hill, washed out by the rain. It was secluded, private, and quiet. Spring was my favorite season because I could see the white blooms of the flowering dogwood trees that represented the cross.

*2. Prayer (22:40–44).* Jesus instructed his disciples in the vital role of prayer. In Luke 22:40, he said, "Pray that you will not fall into temptation" (NIV). Again in verse 46, he told them, "Get up and pray so that you will not fall into temptation" (NIV). He understood their humanity and sympathized with their weaknesses. Of all of the things Jesus could have said in this terrible moment of agony and stress, it all came down to this instruction about prayer. Since he said it twice, we see that it must contain a powerful and intensive truth.

*For reasons we do not know for sure, Judas' enthusiasm for Christ had diminished, and the appeal of money had increased.*

Prayer is the means by which God best gives us his powerful influence and transmits his holy inspiration to motivate us to live above sin and capture the essence of our spiritual life. During and after prayer, the enticement of temptation is more easily defeated and the motivation to overcome is greatly heightened. Clearly, prayer was a means, if not the ultimate means, of perseverance for Jesus. When times are at their darkest and stress is at its highest, maintaining one's spirit of worship through prayer will help guard us against the temptation to give up and give in.

Jesus, having instructed his disciples to pray, then entered into an amazing and unique episode of prayer. His recorded prayer was simple and short. It began with an appeal to a relationship as he called to his "Father" (22:42). Behind the confidence of Christ was a Father who loved his Son and who would be present during the dreadful events ahead.

The "cup" (22:42) refers to that physical, emotional, and spiritual torture of trial and crucifixion that was about to be heaped upon Jesus' body and soul (see Matthew 20:28; John 18:11). What was the "cup"? It was Jesus' total exposure to all the suffering that crucifixion would embody.

Jesus purposefully sought this time of prayer to gain strength in anticipation of the coming pain and sorrow. Though secluded from his disciples, Christ would not hide his feelings from the Father. The agony or "anguish" of the cry for communion with the Father expressed the horror of the coming events (22:44). The forces of hatred, rejection, mockery, pain, and death encircled his spirit with dreadful peril. He prayed with such feeling, grief, and anticipation that his sweat was "like drops of blood falling to the ground" (Luke 22:44, NIV). Nowhere in all of literature is prayer portrayed in such an intense manner. All evidence indicates that this time of prayer was urgent for our Lord in his quest to redeem people from sin.

*3. Purpose (22:42).* The third motivational, strengthening factor was that of purpose. Christ had come to pay the price of people's redemption. Like the seed that must die in order to be fruitful, Jesus accepted the will of God, which meant death. Following the purpose of God for his life was necessary, and this purpose must not be lost over a few hours of physical suffering. At no moment did our Lord depart from the purpose of the Father. He must not and would not. Only if the Father so ordered would Jesus be diverted from fulfilling this purpose. There was no sense of self-pity, no bitterness, no sarcasm, no shrinking from the task, and no

## Judas' Motivation

Judas' motive for betraying Jesus is not known for certain. Here are some possibilities, though.[2]

- Judas' disappointment that Jesus did not strike decisively at the enemies of Israel
- Judas' resentment of Jesus' association with tax collectors and sinners and Jesus' breaking of Jewish traditions
- Judas' disappointment at what he considered to be Jesus' failure to display his power in Jerusalem, so that Judas' betrayal was an attempt to force Jesus to exercise his power and claim his messiahship
- Judas' desire for monetary gain

Which motive do you think was most important? My choice is the last one—greed. All of the other motives could have been achieved without a single coin being exchanged.

denial on the part of Jesus. He looked for no escape other than the Father's will and purpose. He was ready to prove himself and accomplish his purpose in coming.

*4. Providence (22:43).* A fourth motivational force in Jesus' life was providence. "An angel from heaven appeared to him and strengthened him"(22:43, NIV). The power of God, in the form of an angel to give strength, was the Father's answer to the prayer of Jesus. Though Jesus continued to pray, the response of the Father was obvious.

Paul learned the same lesson later when he prayed for the removal of the thorn in the flesh and heard God say, "My grace is sufficient for you . . ." (2 Corinthians 12:9, NIV). God's providence may not prevent a disaster, but it always brings strength and encouragement.

*When times are at their darkest and stress is at its highest, maintaining one's spirit of worship through prayer will help guard us against the temptation to give up and give in.*

The angel was a source of strength for Jesus to go the distance and complete the task. Since the tragedy of Calvary would not be avoided, our Lord found the resources of the Father powerful in reinforcing his resolve and comforting his pain. This is one of the greatest doctrinal truths in Scripture. The key in dealing with tragedy is what we do with tragedy rather than what we allow tragedy to do to us. We do well to remember when facing difficulty that when Jesus ascended, he left his Spirit to comfort us with strength (John 14:15–18). Jesus never promised always to remove the evil, tragedy, illness, or disappointment. He does, always, give his strengthening presence.

## Priorities That Undermine Faithfulness

We face the question about priorities at every crossroad and in every decision. Choosing the wrong priority alters behavior with undeniable force. In this passage in Luke, we can see three wrong priorities that resulted in the undermining of faithfulness.

*Flesh (22:45–46).* The first reason we note in this passage for faithlessness is that of physical frailties of the flesh. All prayerful petitions completed, our Lord got up to find the disciples asleep, worn out from their grief and sorrow. The ability of the disciples to stay alert was hampered by their intense sorrow for their Master and perhaps even for themselves.

Emotional exhaustion can bring physical exhaustion. The human frailties of the body can take so much and then rest must come. Constant sorrow produces a burdensome physical tiredness that demands rest. Eyelids droop, and the body slumps into the relaxed posture of sleep.

*Behind the confidence of Christ was a Father who loved his Son and who would be present during the dreadful events ahead.*

It takes very little to bring sleep to some in church. Almost all Christians "sleep"—literally or symbolically—at inappropriate times, times when Christ is about some of his most serious work. Most of us have little difficulty in understanding how tiredness can bring sleep at the most inopportune moment. Jesus, though, rebuked the disciples for sleeping and encouraged them again to pray. Many other appeals to faithlessness also come to us through our flesh, temptations such as addiction, abuse, gluttony, laziness, and lust. Such weaknesses of the flesh can be stumbling blocks for the soul.

*Financial (22:47–48).* The disciples Jesus led to Gethsemane were not faithful in the hour of stress because of emotional and physical exhaustion. Judas, though, may have weakened to the appeal of money (see John 12:6).

As with the rest of Judas' background and character, Judas' motive in betraying Jesus is vague and puzzling. He was the only Judean of the twelve, and his usefulness in Jesus' ministry can only be assumed. Luke listed him last in the list of apostles (Luke 6:14–16). Judas was the treasurer of this little band of followers. Because of Judas' betrayal of Jesus, the gospels use harsh terms to describe him. John goes so far as to identify him with Satan (John 6:70) and the Antichrist (John 17:12). For reasons we do not know for sure, Judas' enthusiasm for Christ had diminished, and the appeal of money had increased.

*At no moment did our Lord depart from the purpose of the Father.*

Immediately after the strengthening experience of prayer, Jesus was confronted with deceitful betrayal. Judas went to Gethsemane to keep the promise for which he had been paid thirty pieces of silver (see Matthew 26:15). It was probably after midnight, under the cloak of darkness, when Judas, with Temple police and Roman soldiers, came to the quiet garden of prayer. They arrived as Jesus rebuked the sleeping disciples. Judas betrayed Jesus with a greeting of friendship and thus became infamous by his polite betrayal. According to previous arrangement (Matt. 26:48), he identified Jesus with a kiss. Judas' kiss was the kiss of

## Checking My Motivations and Hindrances to Faithfulness

A. Do I have these motivations to faithfulness in my life?

___ 1. A place where I feel especially near to God

___ 2. The regular practice of prayer

___ 3. A stated purpose or mission for my life

___ 4. Recognition that God will keep his promises and provide for me

B. Do any of these hindrances keep me from being faithful?

___ 1. Surrendering to weaknesses of the flesh

___ 2. Desiring money at almost any cost

___ 3. Fearing personal pain and rejection

death for both of them. Had Judas only known that the silver he received would be used to provide a grave, surely he would have acted more wisely (Matt. 27:6–7).

*God's providence may not prevent a disaster, but it always brings strength and encouragement.*

Betrayal of Jesus is not as uncommon as we would like to think. If Judas is to be condemned, then so are all of us who politely greet Jesus and then betray him. Betrayals that involve money, goods, and services are too numerous to count. Betraying Jesus can be involved in such things as subtle as choosing our vocation, selecting a mate, paying the price of a movie ticket, letting anger dominate us, abusing a child, neglecting the poor, choosing abortion, or using drugs. Betrayal can be so subtle that it evades our consciousness. At other times it can be predetermined and calculated. The results that Judas achieved may not be the same as ours, but the sin is no less condemning. Betrayal signifies our spiritual weakness. We can be thankful that the power of God can help us overcome our temptations to betrayal. By his death, Jesus blotted out our insidious betrayals, and we can receive forgiveness as we confess them to him.

Judas may not have expected his betrayal to lead to the death of Jesus. In fact, Judas' dramatic return of the pieces of silver expressed his objection to what he, the Jews, and the Romans had done (see Matt. 27:3). Judas had failed miserably. Judas' suicide showed his sense of shame and guilt.

*Fear (22:54–62).* Jesus was arrested Thursday night. A series of false charges, trials, mockery, and rebuke followed. During the hostility, Peter denied him. Why? Fear—loss of nerve or courage—was the reason. When Luke wrote, "Peter followed at a distance," he may have been preparing us for this cowardly response (22:54, NIV). Luke also tells us that after the fire was kindled, "Peter sat down with them" (22:55, NIV). There at the fireside more for obscurity than for the warmth of the fire, Peter tried to blend in and be one of the background crowd. This act highlights how the situation had intimidated Peter. Though he is to be commended for being in the courtyard of Caiaphas, the high priest, with Jesus, Peter's lack of motivation to remain faithful was already becoming obvious.

Peter's faithlessness was not the same as that of Judas, but could Peter's denials have been even more disappointing for Jesus? Peter had been one of Jesus' first and closest disciples and had known him in ways that Judas had not. Peter had voiced loudly and clearly his determination to be faithful (22:33). In the courtyard of the high priest, Peter had three opportunities to make good on his determination and plead for the cause of the gospel and the ministry of his Lord. Each time, though, Peter thoroughly failed. Notice his replies, in sequence (22:57–58,60, NIV): "Woman, I don't know him"; "Man, I am not!"; and "Man, I don't know what you're talking about!"

*The key in dealing with tragedy is what we do with tragedy rather than what we allow tragedy to do to us.*

Jesus heard Peter's answers, at least the final one, and "looked straight at Peter" (22:61, NIV). Could there be a greater anguish than looking into the penetrating, disappointed eyes of Jesus? Peter had denied Jesus because of fear for his personal well-being. He really could not die for Christ as he had said he would. He did not have the resolve, motivation, courage, or faithfulness to complete his commitment.

Notice, however, that Jesus did not abandon Peter when Peter denied him. Does this contrast not make the death of Christ for us more powerful? Jesus did not betray Peter in his moment of danger. In deepest love, Jesus kept his commitment to the death, by submitting to crucifixion and dying for Peter—and for us.

We can appreciate Peter's fear, can't we? In his impetuousness, he earlier had resisted with the sword and cut off the ear of one of the soldiers. Perhaps as Peter waited in the courtyard, he feared that retaliation might come for that act. He also was very much aware of the antagonism of the

Jewish leaders, for he had experienced their feelings and actions of hatred before. The situation was filled with anger and hostility, and he was without support.

Peter was like many who hide their fears behind bold words of courage. He thoughtlessly sought to lead with his sword or his words. His faithfulness was more for show than for sacrifice. Stepping forward to convince his fellow disciples that he could be counted on, Peter hid his lack of resources for the real confrontation and conflict. His fear was stronger than his resolve.

*Peter's faithlessness was not the same as that of Judas, but could Peter's denials have been even more disappointing for Jesus?*

## Time to Choose

What resources do you need to maintain your faithfulness to Christ? These events in Gethsemane show us the importance of a special place of solitude, prayer with submission, a purpose not to be denied, and the power of God's strengthening presence. These events also call us to examine reasons for our failures in faithfulness. Are we surrendering to weaknesses of the flesh? Do we desire money at almost any cost? Do we fear personal pain? These events remind us that we, too, must choose our priorities wisely if we are to be faithful to Christ.

## QUESTIONS

1. How important is dealing with fear in living out our faithfulness?

2. How can we be certain that we will act faithfully rather than fail unfaithfully?

3. How often do we hide our weaknesses by words of action and strength?

4. Is it better to be unfaithful in deed or in word?

5. How fair is it for us to condemn Peter's denials when our fear of rejection keeps us from witnessing?

6. How do you explain the psychology of hiding our weaknesses behind words of boldness?

7. What are some challenges in your Christian walk that especially bring out your fears? Consider challenges such as tithing, dealing with moral issues, facing personal rejection, or fearing that faithfulness to Christ will cause loss of income.

## NOTES

1. Harry Leon McBeth, *Texas Baptists: A Sesquicentennial History* (Dallas, Texas: BAPTISTWAY Press, 1998), 15.
2. E.P. Blair, "Judas," *The Interpreter's Dictionary of the Bible* (New York: Abingdon Press, 1962), 2:1007.

# How to Order More *Bible Study for Texas*

If you'd like to order more copies of this issue of *Bible Study for Texas,* including a teaching guide, here's how. You can also order other issues of *Bible Study for Texas* as they are released.

Please fill in the following information:

| Title of item | Price | Quantity | Cost |
|---|---|---|---|
| *Luke: Meeting Jesus Again, Anew* | $1.95 | ______ | ______ |
| *Luke: Meeting Jesus Again, Anew* —TEACHING GUIDE | $1.95 | ______ | ______ |
| Available for use beginning June 2000 | | | |
| *Acts: Sharing God's Good News with Everyone* | $1.95 | ______ | ______ |
| *Acts: Sharing God's Good News with Everyone*—TEACHING GUIDE | $1.95 | ______ | ______ |
| Available for use beginning September 2000 | | | |
| *Romans: Good News for a Troubled World* | $1.95 | ______ | ______ |
| *Romans: Good News for a Troubled World* —TEACHING GUIDE | $1.95 | ______ | ______ |
| Available for use beginning December 2000 | | | |
| *God's Message in the Old Testament* | $1.95 | ______ | ______ |
| *God's Message in the Old Testament* —TEACHING GUIDE | $1.95 | ______ | ______ |

| | |
|---|---|
| Subtotal | ______________ |
| Shipping* | ______________ |
| TOTAL | ______________ |

*Charges for standard shipping service:

| | |
|---|---|
| Subtotal up to $20.00 | $3.95 |
| Subtotal $20.01—$50.00 | $4.95 |
| Subtotal $50.01—$100.00 | 10% of subtotal |
| Subtotal $100.01 and up | 8% of subtotal |

For express shipping service:
Call 1–800–355–5285
for information on additional charges.

________________________________________
Your name

________________________________________
Your church

________________________________________
Mailing address

________________________________________
City State Zip code

Cut out or copy this page and mail it
with your check for the total amount to

Sunday School/Discipleship Division
Baptist General Convention of Texas
333 North Washington
Dallas, TX 75246–1798

Call Sunday School/Discipleship Division
toll-free: 1–800–355–5285 (8:30 a.m.–5:00 p.m., M-F)
Internet e-mail address: baptistway@bgct.org
FAX your order anytime to: 214–828–5187

*Thank You!*